Past Masters
General Editor   Keith Thomas

Wyclif

D0845155

Past Masters

AQUINAS Anthony Kenny
ARISTOTLE Jonathan Barnes
BACH Denis Arnold
FRANCIS BACON Anthony Quinton
BAYLE Elisabeth Labrousse
BERKELEY J. O. Urmson
THE BUDDHA Michael Carrithers
BURKE C. B. Macpherson
CARLYLE A. L. Le Quesne
CHAUCER George Kane
CLAUSEWITZ Michael Howard
COBBETT Raymond Williams
COLERIDGE Richard Holmes
CONFUCIUS Raymond Dawson
DANTE George Holmes
DARWIN Jonathan Howard
DIDEROT Peter France
GEORGE ELIOT Rosemary Ashton
ENGELS Terrell Carver
GALILEO Stillman Drake
GIBBON J. W. Burrow
GOETHE T. J. Reed
HEGEL Peter Singer

HOMER Jasper Griffin
HUME A. J. Ayer
JESUS Humphrey Carpenter
KANT Roger Scruton
LAMARCK L. J. Jordanova
LEIBNIZ G. MacDonald Ross
LOCKE John Dunn
MACHIAVELLI Quentin Skinner
MARX Peter Singer
MENDEL Vitezslav Orel
MONTAIGNE Peter Burke
THOMAS MORE Anthony Kenny
WILLIAM MORRIS Peter Stansky
MUHAMMAD Michael Cook
NEWMAN Owen Chadwick
PASCAL Alban Krailsheimer
PETRARCH Nicholas Mann
PLATO R. M. Hare
PROUST Derwent May
RUSKIN George P. Landow
ADAM SMITH D. D. Raphael
TOLSTOY Henry Gifford
WYCLIF Anthony Kenny

Forthcoming

AUGUSTINE Henry Chadwick
BERGSON Leszek Kolakowski
JOSEPH BUTLER R. G. Frey
CERVANTES P. E. Russell
COPERNICUS Owen Gingerich
DESCARTES Tom Sorell
DISRAELI John Vincent
ERASMUS James McConica
GODWIN Alan Ryan
GOETHE T. J. Reed
HERZEN Aileen Kelly
JEFFERSON Jack P. Greene
JOHNSON Pat Rogers
KIERKEGAARD Patrick Gardiner

LEONARDO E. H. Gombrich
LINNAEUS W. T. Stearn
MILL William Thomas
MONTESQUIEU Judith Shklar
NEWTON P. M. Rattansi
ROUSSEAU Robert Wokler
RUSSELL John G. Slater
ST PAUL G. B. Caird
SHAKESPEARE Germaine Greer
SOCRATES Bernard Williams
SPINOZA Roger Scruton
VICO Peter Burke
VIRGIL Jasper Griffin
and others

Anthony Kenny

Wyclif

Oxford   New York

OXFORD UNIVERSITY PRESS

1985

Oxford University Press, Walton Street, Oxford OX2 6DP

London New York Toronto
Delhi Bombay Calcutta Madras Karachi
Kuala Lumpur Singapore Hong Kong Tokyo
Nairobi Dar es Salaam Cape Town
Melbourne Auckland

and associated companies in
Beirut Berlin Ibadan Mexico City Nicosia

Oxford is a trade mark of Oxford University Press

First published 1985 as an Oxford University Press paperback
and simultaneously in a hardback edition

British Library Cataloguing in Publication Data

Kenny, Anthony
Wyclif.—(Past masters)
1. Wycliffe, John
I. Title II. Series
230'.092'4 BX4905

ISBN 0-19-287647-3
ISBN 0-19-287646-5 Pbk

Set by Grove Graphics
Printed in Great Britain by
Cox & Wyman Ltd, Reading

Foreword

John Wyclif was long ago given the title 'Morning Star of the Reformation'. For centuries he has been looked upon by members of the reformed churches as a precursor, a lone voice who spoke for truth and enlightenment in the deepest darkness of the Middle Ages. His attacks on the wealth and corruption of the medieval Church, his denunciation of the antichristian sins of the Papacy, his exposure of the superstitions and idolatries associated with the use of the sacraments, and especially his appeal to scripture as the rule of faith are things which have appealed, and continue to appeal, to all those who are proud to call themselves Protestants. Above all, he is known as the originator of the English Bible; and even if today learned spoilsports claim that he had no more personal hand in the Wycliffe Bible than King James had in the King James Bible, his name is still honoured by the devoted and scholarly Wycliffe Bible Translators who give their lives to the rendering of the scriptures into ever new languages.

It is a truth which has fascinated philosophers that the Morning Star is identical with the Evening Star; and if Wyclif was the Morning Star of the Reformation, he was also the Evening Star of Scholasticism. He belonged to the distinguished line of philosophers and theologians who produced the scholastic system, a synthesis of Christian and Aristotelian ideas which is perhaps the greatest intellectual legacy of the Middle Ages. Wyclif was the last of the great Oxford schoolmen; he is much less known as a philosopher than as a reformer, because those who were interested in his kind of philosophy disowned him as a heretic, and those who hailed him as a forerunner regarded scholastic philosophy as one of the corruptions from which the Reformation offered liberation.

It is the aim of the present book to do justice, so far as the small compass permits, to both sides of Wyclif's achievement: to sketch the mind of a man who combined philosophical insight with reforming zeal, and to invite the reader to reassess his significance in an age in which philosophy has become secularized and theology has become ecumenical.

Contents

Acknowledgements *viii*

Abbreviations *ix*

1 The philosopher of truth *1*

2 Being, form, and essence *18*

3 Freedom and necessity *31*

4 Grace and dominion *42*

5 The truth of scripture *56*

6 Church, King, and Pope *68*

7 The body of Christ *80*

8 The end of the heretic *91*

9 The afterlife of the reformer *100*

Further reading *110*

Index *113*

Acknowledgements

I am indebted to Dr Anne Hudson, Dr Maurice Keen, Dr Jeremy Catto, Professor Paul Spade, Professor Peter Geach, Mr Keith Thomas, and Dr Henry Hardy for help generously given while I was working on this book.

Abbreviations

The following abbreviations are used in page references to Wyclif's works given in the text:

H   *Selections from English Wycliffite writings*, ed. A. Hudson (Cambridge University Press, 1978)

U   *De Universalibus (On Universals)*, ed. I. Mueller, P. Spade, A. Kenny (Oxford University Press, 1984)

W   *Wyclif's Latin Works*, The Wyclif Society, London, 1883–1922, 36 volumes. Individual volumes are cited by the year of publication, as follows:

1883 *Polemical Works*, ed. R. Buddensieg

1885 *De Civili Dominio (On Civil Dominion)*, ed. R. L. Poole

1886 *De Ecclesia (On the Church)*, ed. J. Loserth

1890 *Sermons*, ed. J. Loserth

1892 *De Eucharistia (On the Eucharist)*, ed. J. Loserth

1893 *De Logica (Logical Works)*, ed. M. H. Dziewicki, vol. 1

1899 *De Logica (Logical Works)*, ed. M. H. Dziewicki, vol. 3

1902 *Miscellanea Philosophica (Philosophical Miscellanies)*, ed. M. H. Dziewicki

1905 *De Veritate Sacrae Scripturae (On the Truth of Sacred Scripture)*, ed. Buddensieg, vol. 1

1906 *De Veritate Sacrae Scripturae (On the Truth of Sacred Scripture)*, ed. Buddensieg, vol. 2

1907 *De Potestate Papae (On the Power of the Pope)*, ed. J. Loserth

1910 *Opera Minora (Minor Works)*, ed. J. Loserth

1   The philosopher of truth

Wyclif lived from the late twenties to the early eighties of the fourteenth century. He was a dozen years older than Geoffrey Chaucer, and they had friends in common. His career fell under the last two kings of the main Plantagenet line, Edward III and his grandson Richard II. Because Edward had a long dotage, and Richard succeeded while still a child, the effective ruler of England during much of Wyclif's working life was John of Gaunt, Duke of Lancaster, Edward's son and Richard's uncle. To many people, John of Gaunt is best known for the speech placed on his dying lips in Shakespeare's *Richard II*: the eloquent homage to England which begins 'This royal throne of kings, this sceptred isle!' The real John of Gaunt was more ambitious and less patriotic than Shakespeare's elder statesman; for better or worse, his power and patronage provided the framework for Wyclif's public career.

It was not until 1374 that Wyclif encountered the royal service: for the previous twenty years he had lived a scholarly life at Oxford. He came there, a Yorkshireman born, a few years after the great plague known as the Black Death; the Hundred Years' War between England and France was just coming to the end of its first phase. For more than a century Oxford University had been one of the great centres of European thought: it was entering on a period of comparative independence and isolation from its great sister university at Paris. The best known scholars of the generations before Wyclif, Duns Scotus and William Ockham, had both lectured in Paris as well as in Oxford, and had lived long periods on the Continent; Wyclif except for one brief visit abroad spent all his life in England. University lectures and sermons continued to be in Latin, and almost all Wyclif's works were written in that tongue; but Oxford men now began to write and preach in English too.

In the University which Wyclif entered there were already in existence half a dozen of the colleges which still survive in Oxford: University, Balliol, Merton, Queen's, Exeter, St Edmund Hall. But these colleges were not the powerful institutions within the University which they are today. The University nowadays consists of a confederation of Colleges with a few small religious halls attached: St Benet's, for instance, for Benedictine monks, and Greyfriars for Franciscan friars. To imagine the Oxford of Wyclif's time you must imagine the University of today turned inside out: the most influential institutions in the University were the houses of monks and friars, and the colleges were comparatively insignificant bodies, little grander than the lodging houses in which the majority of the scholars lived.

Most of Oxford's famous sons had been from the religious orders, especially from the 'mendicant' friars, whose vocation called for an austere life supported by the alms they begged. The two best known orders of mendicants were the Dominicans, the preaching friars whose especial care was to preserve the Catholic faith from heresy, and the Franciscans, who pursued ideals of apostolic simplicity and poverty. The unworldly spirituality of the earliest disciples of St Francis was constantly being modified to take account of the realities of ecclesiastical administration. In particular, Franciscans often gave themselves to academic learning. Oxford's first Chancellor, Robert Grosseteste the Bishop of Lincoln, one of Wyclif's lifelong heroes, had been the Franciscans' lecturer; Roger Bacon, the university's first experimental scientist, was a Franciscan. So too were the two most distinguished philosophers and theologians the university had produced, Scotus and Ockham.

It was only in the decades before Wyclif's arrival in Oxford that there began to appear first-rate scholars drawn from the secular or parochial clergy and attached to colleges rather than friaries: men like Thomas Bradwardine and Richard Fitzralph, who were both fellows first of Balliol and then of Merton. Wyclif, like them a secular, followed in their footsteps in the opposite direction: he was a fellow of Merton in the 1350s, and Master of Balliol by 1360.

The course of studies at Oxford in the fourteenth century fell into two parts, and Wyclif was only half-way through his when he became Master of Balliol. The first half was the arts course, which included the liberal arts of grammar, arithmetic, geometry, astronomy, music, and rhetoric; a scholar would be encouraged by his master to concentrate especially on the seventh art, logic. Logic provided the introduction to the study of philosophy; there were three branches of this: natural philosophy (covering the topics now treated by scientific disciplines), moral philosophy or ethics, and metaphysics. The second half of an academic training was a degree course in one of the higher faculties of medicine, law, or theology. When the arts course was successfully completed, which took six or eight years, the candidate became a Master of Arts, which made him a member of the governing body of the University; the second part of the course was crowned when the candidate became a Doctor. Wyclif did not take his Doctorate of theology until 1372, about eighteen years after he first came to Oxford; but he had already been lecturing and writing for many years. Teaching and learning were closely interwoven in the course, from the BA onwards; indeed a Bachelor, in order to become a

Master of Arts, had to give lecture courses for several years.

Lecture courses in Arts were usually attached, more or less loosely, to set texts of Aristotle, but the lecturer was free to concentrate on topics which interested him. One of the most valued methods of instruction, and of examination, was the disputation, in which master or scholar publicly defended, in accordance with strict logical rules, a thesis on a philosophical or theological topic. Disputations were public spectacles, the academic equivalent of a chivalric tournament; in some of their more elaborate forms they were highly stylized, as removed from the cut-and-thrust of spontaneous academic debate as a modern fencing match is from a lethal sword-fight.

The conventions of these scholastic disputations influenced Wyclif's style throughout his life, and his first surviving works are his lecture courses on the logic of the Oxford schools. His *Logic* (W 1893) is a brief treatise on elementary Aristotelian logic; clear and brisk, and free from the repetitions and digressions which were to plague his later works, it contains little that is original. But one feature is notable: he declares that what he is expounding is the logic of sacred scripture; and though the content of the treatise is traditional Aristotelian teaching, very many of the examples used are biblical texts.

The *Continuation of Logic* (W 1893–9) is several times longer than the *Logic*; it is more original, more discursive, and takes sides on matters of contemporary controversy. Thus Wyclif, reacting against the Aristotelian teaching that matter is infinitely divisible, defends a form of atomism. The world, he says, is composed of indivisible atoms; it cannot be increased or reduced in size, or moved or changed in shape.

It is the juxtaposition of atoms, in the appropriate conditions, which truly constitutes the compound . . . Though no bodily eye can recognize the individual positions of the corpuscles in the compound, God knows most distinctly, and the human intellect knows obscurely, what position is to be assigned in each compound. (W 1899. 80)

In other works Wyclif shows his interest in contemporary astronomy and optics: his essay on the *Acts of the Soul* (W 1902) is in part a commentary on a treatise on perspective by the Polish optician Witelo.

The natural philosophy of the fourteenth century has been almost entirely antiquated by the progress of science. It is often interesting to see how many of the ideas of Galileo, Newton, and others were anticipated in medieval Oxford, but the interest is historical rather than philosophical. It is another matter with medieval logic and metaphysics: here the scholars and students of the fourteenth century were discussing problems and using methods which are current among Oxford philosophers today.

In the mid-twentieth century, as in the mid-fourteenth, philosophers in Oxford pay keen attention to the nature of language: to the way in which terms have meaning, the way in which sentences are put together, the way in which human beings do things with words. In this, contemporary Oxford philosophy resembles the philosophy of Wyclif's day more than it resembles the Oxford of the nineteenth century or the Paris of the twentieth century. Like Wyclif's philosophy, Oxford philosophy today is linguistic philosophy in the sense that it regards the study of language as a central and powerful method for the solution of philosophical problems and the pursuit of philosophical enlightenment.

One can believe that philosophy is linguistic in this sense without believing that philosophy is only *about* language. Among philosophers who are linguistic in the broad sense of using linguistic methods there is keen debate today whether philosophy is linguistic in the narrow sense of being concerned only with language, and not with the world. This debate is raised in various forms: it is often called a debate between realists and anti-realists. Philosophers ask, for instance, whether truth is objective: is our understanding of language based on an absolute conception of truth itself as opposed to our methods of discovering truth and expressing it? A popular view at the present time is one which may be called creative anti-realism: according to this it is human thought and language that are somehow responsible for the ultimate structure of reality. At the other extreme there are realists who claim that the fundamental framework not only of the actual world, but of all possible worlds, is something quite independent of any mind, human or divine. Anti-realists clearly assign language a role which goes far beyond anything attributed to it by realists; but both realists and anti-realists are, in the broad sense, 'linguistic philosophers' and belong to the tradition dominant nowadays in Oxford and most of the English-speaking world.

The conflict between realism and anti-realism mirrors a conflict which was being conducted among the scholastic philosophers of the fourteenth century. Both Wyclif and his immediate predecessors were linguistic philosophers in the sense that they paid great attention to language; but the great philosophers of the previous generation, such as Ockham, defended a form of anti-realism, known as nominalism, whereas Wyclif himself was a realist. The form which the argument took was a debate over the nature of universals.

What is a universal? Take a word such as 'animal'. This is a term which is universal in the sense that it can be applied to many different things. It is not a proper name like 'Bucephalus'; it can be used of the cat Tibbles and of the dog Fido and of the man John. Now what, in reality, corresponds to this universal term? What is it that John and Fido and Tibbles have in common which makes them all animals? Shall we say that they have nothing in common except the fact that we use the same name 'animal' to refer to each of them? But surely that is absurd. Surely it is because they are all animals that we can call them by the same name, not the other way round! So they must have something in common in reality. But what is that common thing they share? Is it itself an animal? If not, how can it be something which we can rightly refer to by the word 'animal'? If it is, then must it not be a fourth animal, an animal distinct from John and Fido and Tibbles, since none of them can be identified with each other? But is not such a fourth animal, in its turn, something absurd in itself: an animal that is common to every animal and yet distinct from any of them?

The problem of accounting for the meaning of general terms is a key problem in the philosophy of language. From one point of view, which Wyclif shared with many of his contemporaries, this problem, the problem of universals, can appear as *the* problem of philosophy. The first of the answers suggested above, the answer that objects have nothing in common other than the names we attach to them, is the *nominalist* answer; the second answer, that there is in the real world something which is common to all things of a kind but distinct from any of them, is the *realist* answer. Hardly any philosopher has presented either the nominalist or the realist answer in the extreme form presented above; but in the fourteenth century as at the present day philosophers tend towards one or other of the two poles on this issue. Wyclif saw it as his major philosophical task to undertake the defence of realism against nominalism.

Historians of philosophy and theology have fostered the idea that in the Middle Ages realism belonged with Catholic orthodoxy and that it was the growth of nominalism which paved the way for the Protestant Reformation. But this association is too facile, as is shown by Wyclif's own career: an arch-heretic in his later life, he was at all times a passionate realist. Wyclif would indeed have agreed that nominalism leads to heresy; he thought it incompatible with an orthodox grasp of the Trinity. He believed that he and his friends had been raised up by God to defend realism against the nominalism of the previous generation so that the true Christian doctrine would not die out. His great adversary, in the early part of his career, was Ockham, who had denied realist universals, stressed an empiricist theory of knowledge, and endeavoured to interpret metaphysical truths as truths about language. He attacked Ockham's 'modernism', and mocked his disciples as 'doctors of signs': they remain fixed for lifetime in the first stages of grammar.

Wyclif wrote as if he had been brought up as a nominalist, and as if it was the dominant tendency in the Oxford of his time; but in attacking it he was aligning himself with conservative orthodoxy. Fifty-one points of Ockham's teaching had been censured at the Papal court at Avignon in 1326, and nominalist techniques which were believed to lead to sceptical doubts were condemned several times in the University of Paris in the 1330s and '40s.

Wyclif's major philosophical work, which occupied him

from about 1365 to 1372, was the *Summa de Ente*, a compendium of philosophical questions in thirteen treatises grouped into two books. The title of the work stresses its comprehensiveness: *'Ens'*, which means 'being' or 'entity', is the most general word in medieval Latin for all that there is. The first book, of seven treatises, considers being in relation to man; the second book, with six treatises, considers God and his attributes – understanding, knowledge, will, and creative power. When, in the second book, Wyclif comes to treat of the Trinity and of the divine Ideas, he crosses the boundary between philosophy (including philosophy of religion or natural theology) and theology strictly so called (specifically Christian or 'revealed' theology). It may well be that these treatises mark Wyclif's first lectures in the theology faculty.

The *Summa de Ente* has never been published as a whole. Three of the treatises of the first part were published by the Wyclif Society (W 1901 and 1909); two were published in a separate edition in 1930 after the Society had ceased to function. The most important of the philosophical treatises, the one on Universals, had to wait for publication until the sexcentenary year of 1984; the seventh treatise, concerning time, is being prepared for publication. Only two treatises of the second book have been published (W 1909); the remainder of the work still awaits an editor.

As a sample of Wyclif's philosophical thought, we shall consider the treatment of nominalism and realism from the treatise on Universals in the first book. This work was early recognized as central to Wyclif's philosophy, as appears from the unusually large number of manuscripts in which it has been preserved; it also looks forward in several ways to the reformer's radical theological thought.

The treatise is impressive. Wyclif draws on a wide

variety of sources, and organizes them into a lively and individual whole. Like any scholastic, he quotes copiously from the works of Aristotle; but in invoking his authority he is not at all servile. He disagrees with him from time to time, and points out that as a pagan the philosopher was ignorant of many truths which Christians know. He makes use of Arabic commentaries on Aristotle, such as the works of Averroës and Avicenna, which he knew, like the text of Aristotle, in Latin versions. Among Christian authors he quotes most voluminously from St Augustine, treating him with veneration and careful never to disagree with him; only Grosseteste and St Anselm of Canterbury receive a comparable degree of respect. Standard scholastic authorities such as St Thomas Aquinas and Duns Scotus are referred to politely; so too are more recent authors like Bradwardine and Fitzralph, and another predecessor at Balliol and Merton, Walter Burley, who is held up as a solid champion of universals. But most scholars from Ockham onwards are denounced, usually anonymously, as 'doctors of signs' who tried to abolish universals and turn the eternal truths of metaphysics into linguistic truisms.

The nominalists' disdain for universals is not a merely academic error, according to Wyclif:

All envy or actual sin is caused by the lack of an ordered love of universals . . . because every such sin consists in a will preferring a lesser good to a greater good, whereas in general the more universal goods are better . . . Thus, if proprietors who are devoted to particulars were more concerned with the well-being of the commonwealth than with the prosperity of their kinsfolk they would not press for their own people to be raised to wealth, office, prelacy and other dignities . . . Beyond doubt,

intellectual and emotional error about universals is the
cause of all the sin that reigns in the world. (U 77)

Thus the germ of Wyclif's later communism is already
found in his logic.

The nominalists, Wyclif maintains, mistake the nature
of universals because they misunderstand the nature of
predication. Universal terms occur as predicates in
sentences. Thus, in 'John is a man' there occurs the term
'man' which tells you what species John belongs to; and in
'John is an animal' there occurs the term 'animal' which
tells you what genus John belongs to – a genus which
includes other species, such as the species *dog, cat*, and so
on. Now nothing can be a predicate – so the nominalists
argue – unless it is a part of a proposition or sentence. But
nothing in the real world is a part of a sentence, so nothing
in the real world is a predicate. So universals, such as
species and genera, are not parts of the real world; being
predicates, they are terms, and terms which do not signify
anything in the world. Thus argue the nominalists.

This is quite wrong, Wyclif argues. Besides a sentence
such as 'John is a man' or 'John is wise', which expresses
a certain truth, we have to look in the world for the truth
it expresses. The sentence does not contain its own truth;
in itself a sentence is just the same whether it is true or
false. To tell whether it is true we have to look outside it
at what corresponds to it in the world. This Wyclif calls,
following Walter Burley, 'the real proposition': it is a
proposition put together by God from subject and
predicate. That is to say, the sentence 'John is wise', which
consists of the subject term 'John' attached to a verbal
predicate, is true only if in the real world the substance John
has attached to itself the characterization *being wise* which
corresponds to the predicate of the sentence. This

11

characterization, Wyclif says, is a form, the form of wisdom; a form which inheres in every individual who is wise. Similarly corresponding to the predicate in the sentence 'John is a man' there is in the world the form of humanity, which inheres in every individual of the human race or species.

So as well as terms which are predicated of individuals, there are forms; forms are predicated of, or are shared by, or are common to individuals. This is the real predication of which predication in language is just a sign. Wyclif has no difficulty in finding passages in Aristotle which support this notion of real predication. Thus in his *Categories* Aristotle had distinguished between primary substances (such as this man, this horse) and secondary substances, which he said were the kinds in which primary substances came. Secondary substance, unlike primary substance, Aristotle said, is said or predicated of a subject. 'This', Wyclif observes, 'is more easily understood about things signified than about their signs.'

It is absurd to say that the existence of species and genera depends upon the mind, at least if the mind we are thinking of is the human mind.

> Even though no created nature ever did any thinking, none the less there would be species and genera truly shared by their individuals; thus it does not depend on any created intellect that it is common to every fire to be fire, and so with the other substances. (U 79)

No doubt universality depends on the mind in the sense that it is the divine intellect of the creator which has produced the common humanity which is shared by each individual human; but being man is common to every man whether or not any creature thinks of this or not.

A correct understanding of predication, Wyclif

maintains, will enable us to see how much better a realist definition of universals is than a nominalist one. A realist will tell us simply that a genus is what is predicated of many things which are different in species. A nominalist has to entangle himself in some circumlocution such as this: 'A genus is a term which is predicable, or whose counterpart is predicable, of many terms which signify things which are specifically distinct.' The nominalist cannot say that it is essential to a term to be actually predicated: perhaps there is no one around to do any verbal predicating. He cannot say that any particular term – any particular sound or image or mark on paper – has to be predicable; most signs do not last long enough for multiple predication. That is why he has to speak of counterparts, that is to say of other resembling signs. He cannot say that the term is predicated of terms differing in species: the *word* 'dog' does not differ in species from the *word* 'cat'; they are both English nouns on this page. So they have to say that the terms *signify* things that differ specifically. But of course in doing this they give the game away: they are making specific difference something on the side of the things signified, not something belonging purely to the signs. So the nominalist's gobbledygook does not really help him at all.

When we talk of species and genus, we are not talking of ink blots on paper; if we were, we could change a man into a donkey by altering the significance of a term. But of course we cannot alter the species and genus of things by fiat, as we can alter the meanings of words by convention. It is not the possibility or the fact of assigning a word which causes extra-mental things to resemble each other more or less; the specific resemblance or difference between things is based on the constituents of things themselves. The predication or predicability of signs is not the reason for the resemblances between extra-mental things; it is the other way round.

So far Wyclif seems to have the better of the argument with his adversary, whether or not the adversary he sets up for himself is a fair representation of Ockham and his disciples. But if his theory is to be not only true but also Aristotelian, what is he to make of the polemic which Aristotle conducted against Plato's theory of Ideas, in a number of passages which Wyclif quotes? For was not Plato's theory nothing other than the postulation of real universals such as the nominalists rejected?

Wyclif knew Plato only at second hand, through Aristotle's critique and Augustine's defence of Platonism. He endeavours to reconcile the two great classical philosophers by making distinctions between different kinds of universals.

First of all, in the mind of God from all eternity there is the thought of all the different kinds of things he can make: these are the patterns and paradigms by which he creates. To refer to these Wyclif, like other Latin theologians, used the Greek word 'Idea'.

The divine Ideas existed from all eternity, and would exist whether or not the world was created. But once things have been created there is another kind of universal: the form which is shared or held in common by all the individuals of a kind. This, Wyclif maintains, is what Aristotle means by genera and species; he calls them metaphysical universals.

Metaphysical universals have in common that they share in universality: they all fall under the concept 'universal'. But this is something which it takes an abstractive intellect to grasp. A dog may recognize another dog as being of its kind; but only a human being can realize that caninity, like humanity, is a universal. Hence universals, considered precisely as universals, have a

14

universality which is introduced by the intellect. Here Wyclif speaks of logical universals.

Finally, there are the words and thoughts which are the signs of universals; these are the universal terms which even the nominalists recognize.

Now if we interpret Plato charitably, we can take it that the ideas he spoke of are the Ideas in the divine mind; and none of Aristotle's arguments suffices to refute the possibility of such Ideas. But what Aristotle is really taking issue with is the notion that there are ideas which are self-subsistent substances, separate from God and from individuals. These, Wyclif agrees, would be unintelligible and superfluous monstrosities. Whether Plato believed in such entities, Wyclif leaves open; but even Aristotle believed that there were forms and natures common to individuals; and these are universals in the second sense listed above, the metaphysical universals.

But what are these universals? What kinds of entities are they? Wyclif explains that the way to understand this is to reflect on the nature of truth. For anyone who grasps a necessary truth already conceives a universal. This seems difficult to accept: how can a universal, which on Wyclif's account is a reality which corresponds to a predicate, be the same as a truth, which is something corresponding to a whole sentence consisting of subject plus predicate? Wyclif agrees that a sentence is complex while a term is not; but he denies that this presents a real difficulty for his thesis. The contrast between complexity and non-complexity is something which belongs to our conceiving, and not to what we conceive.

What Wyclif has in mind seems to be something like this. Suppose that the mind is aware that an individual A resembles an individual B. There must be a particular respect in which A resembles B, since things can be similar

15

in one respect while at the same time dissimilar in another respect – there is no such thing as pure similarity, similarity which is not similarity in some respect. Let us call this respect C: what the mind is aware of is then that A resembles B in respect of C. In seeing the resemblance of A and B in this respect, the mind is seeing the C-ness of A and B; that is to say, it is conceiving C-ness, where 'C' is the name of a universal. Seeing *that A is like B in respect of C* is the very same thing as seeing *the C-ness* of A and B; so what is indicated by the complex clause in the first expression must be the same as what is indicated by the abstract noun in the second. Hence, to grasp a universal is simply to conceive in a non-complex manner what one grasps by a judgement containing a subject and predicate; and anyone who can make judgements of likeness automatically knows what a universal is.

Nominalists attack realists by claiming that the postulation of universals leads to absurd consequences. If there are more men in the world today than there were yesterday, does that mean that the universal man has grown? How many heads does the universal animal have? Does the human species sin? Can it laugh? Are universals created by God? In other chapters of his treatise Wyclif patiently unravels such difficulties, and shows how non-absurd and non-arbitrary answers can be given to these and similar trick questions. In general he deals with the objections successfully, and leaves the reader with the conviction that he has had the better of his nominalist adversaries.

He is less convincing, though sometimes engaging, when he tries to show that a right understanding of universals has beneficial moral effects. He enlists Augustine in support of the thesis that nominalism leads to selfishness, and realism to love of one's neighbour. Real love of one's neighbour must be based on the fact that he or she is a human being, not that he is one's son or she is one's mistress: the common humanity is the work of God, the particular relationship is of one's own making. So every Christian ought to love his neighbour in his common nature, rather than with an eye to individual utility, kinship, or pleasure. How can he do this without a grasp of what is common, the universal humanity? It is a greater good, and a greater object of concern to God, that there should be human beings at all, than that there should be any particular individual. 'So, if I am to conform my will to the divine will, I have a duty to love the superior truth more than the inferior truth.'

2   Being, form, and essence

In Wyclif's philosophy, as in all medieval philosophy, a
central place is occupied by the concept of being. The word
'being' corresponds to the Latin word '*esse*', the infinitive
form of the Latin verb 'to be'. Being, so medievals believed,
is the subject-matter of metaphysics, which was regarded
as the highest branch of philosophy. Metaphysics tells us
what kinds of things there are, and what this being is which
they all share: it tells us what we mean when we say of
things that they are.

Whatever there is, for Wyclif, is an entity (*ens*) and every
entity has being (*esse*). Being is indeed the actuality of
entity: that is to say, being is what an entity does, just as
running is what a runner does. Being is not the same as
existence; there are some things which are, or have being,
and yet do not exist. Indeed, for Wyclif, there are four kinds
of being, of which existence is only one.

The first kind of being which a creature may have is as
an Idea in the mind of God. The most exalted being of
creatures, Wyclif says,

> is the eternal mental being which they have in God.
> Every such being is an item of divine life, and is in reality
> God himself, according to the text of John 1, 'What was
> made, in Him was life'. (U 126)

Secondly, Wyclif says, creatures have being in their
causes whether general or particular. This is called
essential being. When the world began, God made different
kinds, or species; once a species is created, every individual
of that species has one type of being in the species as its

18

universal cause. Again, since, according to Christian teaching, all men not only belong to the same species, but descend from the same stock, all human beings also have a kind of being in the first man as their particular cause. 'In this sense the saints say that the whole human race was the first Adam' (U 127). Thus, all humans who ever have lived or will live have this second kind of being (a) in humankind, (b) in Adam.

There is a third kind of being, and only this being is equivalent to existence.

> Thirdly, creatures have a being which is the existence of the individual, which begins to be and ceases to be at its own time. This is the only being which modern doctors accept. But even recent writers grant, with respect to the second being, that even when there are no roses in existence a rose is a flower . . . For it is one thing to be, and another to exist. (U 127)

The fourth mode of being is the accidental being of a substance: that is to say, the possession by a substance of a non-essential property. In this sense, a man's *being sunburnt* is one of his modes of being. As the example shows, an accidental being of this kind is something that can come and go during the lifetime of the subject, whereas the being of a subject in the third sense, its existence, precisely is its lifetime.

Thus, in Wyclif's system, every creature can have four kinds of being: ideal being in the mind of God; essential being in its causes; existential being or existence in itself; and accidental being in its transitory properties.

The last two kinds of being are not too difficult to understand: the notion of existence and the notion of bearing properties are notions which occur in one form or another in every system of philosophy. Again, anyone who accepts the existence of an omniscient God must agree that whatever there is is in some sense in the mind of God. But why does Wyclif introduce his second kind of being, essential being in causes?

To grasp this we have to recall that Wyclif insisted that the way into metaphysics is to take a firm grasp on the notion of truth. We must ask what is it that makes propositions true: what makes the difference between true propositions and false propositions? The only general answer we can give to that question is: being. It is what there is and what there is not, in the real world, which decides which propositions are true and which false. So the classification of the four kinds of being is at the same time an analysis of four kinds of things in the world that make propositions true or false.

Now among the propositions whose truth we wish to account for there are two particularly important classes of propositions. There are propositions telling us the species and genus to which things belong, and the relationships between these species and genera. Also, there are propositions about the causal relationships between individuals at different times of the world's history. Undoubtedly, we know a number of propositions of these kinds; as that any rose is a flower, and that all men are sons of Adam. How are we to account for the truth of these propositions? What is the being which lies behind their truth?

We cannot say that the truth of these propositions depends on the existence of any individual roses or men. In the first case 'a rose is a flower' remains true even if all roses, sadly, have been destroyed in some cosmic catastrophe. Moreover, even if I say of a particular specimen in my hand 'This is a rose', what I am saying goes beyond the existence of the individual: I am talking about its relationship to its species. This is a relationship which it shares with every other member of the species, but which cannot be reduced to a relationship with the actual existing roses, since new roses are always possible. In the case of the second example 'All men are sons of Adam', the truth expressed cannot be regarded as a truth about a set of existing individuals; for there was never a time when the individuals the proposition is about all existed together to have things true about them. (One might say, no doubt, that things can have relationships at times when they do not exist; and that it is these relationships that the propositions are about. In that case, a relationship of this kind will simply be an instance of what Wyclif calls 'essential being'.) The being, therefore, which gives truth to these propositions cannot be existential being; it is essential being.

What Wyclif means by 'essence' or 'essential being' is not the same as what other philosophers have meant by the term 'essence'. In the usage of many philosophers, a thing's essence is its defining feature, a property which makes it the kind of thing it is, and which it cannot lose without ceasing to exist. Thus, scholastic philosophers would say that Socrates' essence was his humanity or human nature. Wyclif does accept this concept, but he uses to express it not the word 'essence', but the word 'quiddity' (literally 'whatness', i.e. that which makes a thing what it is). For Wyclif, a thing's essence is something of a more general and abstract kind than its quiddity: it is its being an item in the fabric of the universe, its membership of the real world. Thus Socrates' quiddity is what makes him a man rather than a cat; his essence is what makes him a part of history rather than fiction. As Wyclif puts it:

Just as a thing is an entity before it is any kind of thing, and a man is an entity before he is a substance so too it seems that essence, the putting of the bare question 'Is there such a thing?' precedes the quiddity which adds genus to being. (U 130)

We can attach to individuals predicates of ever diminishing generality. Thus we can say of Socrates that he is an entity; he is a substance, not an accident; he is a body, not a spirit; he is living, not inert; he is an animal, not a plant; he is a human being, not a brute beast. This hierarchical ordering should not be misunderstood: nothing could be an animal without being some kind of animal; and 'entity' is not a supreme genus, since it does not say what kind of a thing something is. But there is an ordering between the items listed: if there is such a thing as man, then there is such a thing as animal (since a man is, by definition, a rational animal); but the converse is not the case; there could be and perhaps there once were animals without there being any such thing as men.

One of the ways in which twentieth-century logic differs from fourteenth-century logic is in its treatment of existence. Nowadays, a sentence such as 'God exists' is not regarded, as Wyclif would have regarded it, as having 'God' as a subject and 'exists' as a predicate. Existence is not represented by a predicate but by a quantifier. 'God exists', that is to say, is reformulated as 'For some x, x is God', where 'x' is a variable which keeps a place for a symbol such as a proper name, and 'For some x' is called the existential quantifier.

The use of this symbolism enables one to avoid some confusions in thinking about existence. It frees us, for instance, from the temptation to think that we need somehow to postulate God's existence in order to deny it, lest otherwise there should be no reference for the subject in the sentence 'God does not exist', and thus the whole sentence might lose its meaning.

But it is a mistake to conclude, as is sometimes done, that medieval treatments of being are rendered otiose by the modern use of the quantifier to express existence. Existence, as we have seen, is only one of the four kinds of being distinguished by Wyclif.

The questions which are raised by the other kinds of being are questions which remain quite unclarified by the introduction of the quantifier. For instance, in 'For some x, x is God' what is the status of the predicate '. . . is God'? Does anything in the real world correspond to it? If so, what? Clearly not God, since the sentence must mean the same whether it is true or false; and if the sentence is false there is not any God in the real world. Must there be, then, corresponding to the predicate, some more abstract, universal entity, such as Godhead or divinity? Whatever the correct answer to this question, it is clearly the same question as Wyclif debated with Ockham.

Again, there is the question what kinds of names can be substituted for the variable 'x' in the quantified statement. Is it names only of actual objects or also of possible objects? The enquiry whether there are merely possible objects, and if so, what can be said of them, has become a prime concern of logicians and philosophers in the English-speaking world in the last decades. The enquiry is precisely into the subject-matter which Wyclif called 'essential being'.

Having explained what Wyclif means by 'being', 'entity', 'essence', and 'existence', we must ask what are the relationships between these notions. One of the theses to which Wyclif attaches most importance is this: each thing is the same as its being. What are we to make of this puzzling claim?

Though the thesis is surprising in a medieval context, students of philosophy have long been familiar with a parallel claim in the rather different framework of Hume's discussion of the idea of existence. In the *Treatise of Human Nature* Hume wrote:

> 'Tis also evident, that the idea of existence is nothing different from the idea of any object, and that when after the simple conception of any thing we wou'd conceive it as existent, we in reality make no addition to or alteration on our first idea. Thus when we affirm, that God is existent, we simply form the idea of such a being, as he is represented to us; nor is the existence, which we attribute to him, conceiv'd by a particular idea, which we join to the idea of his other qualities, and can again separate and distinguish from them.

But if Wyclif's thesis has a familiar ring, the arguments by which he seeks to establish it often seem bizarre. First, he attempts to prove the proposition in the case of God, by arguments such as the following:

> If there is a God, then there being a God is something there is. But it is consistent with the antecedent that there should be God alone, that is that there should be no essence or nature other than God; therefore this is consistent also with the consequent, that God's being is something there is. But on the supposition that there is only God, there is no other essence left to stand behind the divine being. In that case therefore that being would be the divine essence. (U 117)

Once established that God is the same as God's being, Wyclif says it follows by similar means that man is the same as there being such a thing as man, and similarly for any other creature.

Other philosophers have maintained that in God there was no distinction between being and essence, and would have agreed that God was identical with God's being. But why does Wyclif believe that what goes for God goes also for any creature?

The key is given by Wyclif's theory of predication, and the clue is given, in the passage just quoted, by his saying that if there is only God 'there is no other essence left to stand behind the divine being'. Once again, Wyclif is looking for what it is that makes propositions true. Now what makes true the proposition 'God is' or 'God has being' is the divine essence; and the divine essence is what is signified by the word 'God'; and this is the sense in which God is God's being, namely, that what 'God' refers to is the same item in the real world as what makes 'God is' true. And we are not dealing here with something that is a mysterious feature peculiar to the divine; it is equally true that what, in the real world, is signified by 'gold' is the very same thing as makes true the proposition 'there is such a thing as gold'. And that is what is meant by saying that gold is gold's being.

But there is no denying that 'gold is gold's being' is a rather odd kind of sentence. Wyclif does not wish to deny this: indeed he coins a special name for that particular kind of sentence: he calls it 'essential predication'. He tells us that there are three chief kinds of predication: formal predication, habitudinal predication, and essential predication. Formal predication is the straightforward kind which occurs in 'snow is white'; it is called formal because it indicates the inherence of the form, whiteness, in the substance snow. Habitudinal predication occurs when a predicate comes to be true of a subject without any change in the subject. (Thus, when Dante falls in love with Beatrice, 'Beatrice is beloved' becomes true, but the change which takes place takes place in Dante not Beatrice; there is no new real predication attaching to Beatrice.) Essential predication is defined as 'predication in which the same essence is the subject and predicate, even though the notion of the predicate differs from the notion of the subject' (U 30). An instance of essential predication would be 'Steam is (the same thing as) ice' – not that being steam is the same as being ice, or that anything could be both at the same time, but, as Wyclif would put it, the same essence which is at one time steam is at another time ice.

The way in which Wyclif's classification of predicates works is this. Given a sentence, you ask what is the item in the real world which verifies it if it is true – remembering that, for Wyclif, the real world contains universals as well as individuals. In a sentence like 'snow is white', what verifies it is a form, the whiteness of snow; this is a formal predication. In a sentence like 'Beatrice is beloved' what verifies it is not anything referred to in the sentence at all; that is habitudinal predication. But in other cases it will be something in which one of the forms mentioned in the sentence inheres or has its being: and in that case it will be essential predication. The essence involved in an essential predication will be that item in the history of the real universe which makes the sentence true, if it is true. The essence in question is what the sentence is *about*.

Wyclif's theory leads to some surprising results. Though all entities have being, not all of them have, or are, essences. Negative items such as privations (e.g. blindness) or sins (e.g. adultery) do not have essences of their own; they are lacks, not positive realities. What then is the essence involved in a predication such as 'David committed adultery'? Wyclif answers:

Though being, in formal predication, is of wider extent

than essence, however, every being is essence either in
formal or essential predication; thus sin in an analogous
sense may mean the sinning subject or the matter on
which is based that which is sin formally so called.
(U 49)

Thus the essence involved in the sentence quoted is David
himself, or, if you like, David's act of copulation, the
material action which, because of its irregular nature, is
formally sin.

A proposition such as 'Socrates is wise' is a straightforward formal predication. But what of propositions such
as 'Socrates is not wise', 'Socrates may be wise some day',
'Socrates was wise once'? We cannot say these are formal
predications; for if they are true there is not, or need not be,
any such form as the wisdom of Socrates to make them
true. Wyclif's answer is startling: 'Truths about the past or
the future, truths about possibility and negations are
essentially God himself' (U 49).

Wyclif is not saying simply that only God *knows* the
future; he is saying that the only truth about the future
there is to know is the divine plan for the future. So too with
the past: the truth that now remains of the past is simply
the plans of God that were executed in the past. And the
truth lying behind negations and possibilities is simply the
power of God to do otherwise than he in fact does. This is
a striking doctrine: and it does not seem to follow after the
careful distinctions Wyclif has drawn between different
types of being. Why should we not say instead, for instance,
that the truth of past and future consists in the essential
being which links them causally to items now in existence?
Perhaps Wyclif would reply that this will only cover events
which are necessitated in the future by present trends, or
events which were the only possible antecedents of present

states of affairs: it will not allow for past and future events which are only contingently or fortuitously linked with the present.

Wyclif maintains that his theory of being and essence is not inconsistent with the standard scholastic teaching that in the case of individual creatures being is not the same as essence.

> Even though every being is essence, and contrariwise, however in every creature being and essence are distinct from each other. (U 49)

For being is essence only if the 'is' is the 'is' of essential predication, not of formal predication; and the distinction between being and essence is obvious

> because every creature has many kinds of being, at least one of which is distinct from essence. Take a given Peter: it is certain that his ideal being is distinct from his particular essence. And again his particular existence is distinct from his quidditative essence in species or genus. (U 128)

From his theory of being and truth Wyclif draws further support for his postulation of universals. Anyone who denies universals in the real world gets into an inextricable tangle because he is denying truth in the real world. How can we allow the nominalists to tell us that a universal is a mere nothing? 'It makes no sense to say that a thing so necessary, so needed by God if we are to share with him, so loved and preserved by God, should be a mere nothing.' Indeed, the nominalists are hoist with their own petard: for is not 'nothing' itself a universal term?

One of the most important conclusions which Wyclif drew from this theory of being was that there was something incoherent in the notion of annihilation.

Individuals certainly go out of existence, just as they come into existence; but in the normal course of events, they go out of existence by being destroyed or perishing, not by being annihilated. They turn into other things, they don't vanish into nothingness. So much was common ground to Wyclif's colleagues. But some argued that God, by his almighty power, could annihilate substances; and they attached such importance to this doctrine that they argued that if the theory of universals was incompatible with the possibility of annihilation, that was by itself enough to refute the theory (U 301).

Wyclif deals with their arguments at great length. His most important contention was that in order to annihilate something, God would have to take away not only its existence, but also every kind of being that it has. But that would be absurd: how could even God take away the being that it has in the divine mind? That would be for God to deny his own omniscience. This is something which the believers in annihilation might agree to: by annihilation, they might reply, they mean only the removal of all creaturely being. But even this is something which Wyclif, because of his theory of being and of universals, cannot allow. Whatever loses its existence retains its essential being: its relationship to the species to which it belongs, and its place in the causal web of the universe. Whatever happens to the individual, this cannot be obliterated without the whole universe being annihilated.

If one studies Wyclif's theology of being, one realizes that his opposition to the notion of annihilation was in essence an affirmation of the view that every item in the universe belongs in a single unbroken system of general laws and causal relationships. To envisage the annihilation of an individual substance would be to break that system and render it unintelligible as a whole. A view like Wyclif's lies behind the whole development of classical physics, and it is something which, to this day, is taken for granted most of the time. But it was something for which Wyclif had to battle, and in his writings there jostle together arguments in its favour with a surprisingly scientific ring, and others with a weirdly archaic theological clangour.

3 Freedom and necessity

One of the heresies for which Wyclif was condemned after his death was the doctrine that everything happens by absolute necessity. As a result of this condemnation, he has been reputed an extreme determinist, and his theory of the relationship between the power of God and the acts of men has often been described as a rigid predestinarianism. But in fact the theory of necessity contained in his philosophical writings was a carefully nuanced one; his system left as much room for human freedom as that of any comparable theologian. Wyclif's affirmation of predestination was no stronger than that of many Catholic thinkers, and he tried to show that it was perfectly compatible with a continuing belief in the freedom of the will.

Wyclif's treatise on logic, like all such textbooks, contained a chapter on necessity and possibility. The term 'necessary', he says, is applied to a truth which cannot not be the case, like 'I am not a donkey'. There are some things which are absolutely necessary and these come in two kinds. A truth of geometry or a proposition such as 'God exists' is *per se* necessary, in the sense that it neither can, nor ever could, nor ever will be able not to be the case. A proposition like 'I have existed for some time' is absolutely necessary too, but only *per accidens*: it cannot now fail to be the case, but it need not have been the case.

There are other things that are necessary, but not absolutely necessary, only conditionally or hypothetically necessary: for instance, the heating of a cold body when a heating agent is applied. We might say that, given the presence of the heating agent, 'This body will be heated' is conditionally necessary; or we might say that the conditional 'If this agent is present, this body will be heated' is necessary. The point can be put either way, but Wyclif prefers to put it in the former way.

Conditional or hypothetical necessity, in its turn, comes in various kinds. The condition may be an antecedent of the event in question; or it may be a consequence of the event; or it may be an accompaniment of the event. The most important kind is where the condition is an antecedent: this is antecedent conditional necessity. Wyclif goes on:

> There is a further threefold subdivision of antecedent necessity. One kind of such necessity is the necessity of volition: as where the unconstrained will of myself or of God is a cause which necessitates something else. Another is natural necessity, as when the application of fire in sufficient force to combustible material acts or begins to act. The third, the necessity of constraint, is the necessity by which a brigand compels his captive to purchase his ransom: this is a mark of helplessness. These two latter necessities remove freedom from what is necessitated in this way. (W 1893. 158)

These distinctions are fairly standard among medieval authors. What is interesting is the way in which in *On Universals* Wyclif applies his distinctions to the vexed problem of the relationship between divine power and human freedom.

He maintained, as we have seen, that every creature is eternally in God, and, once the world has begun, in all its created causes. He now puts the question whether this means that everything happens necessarily. In answering the question, he at once appeals to his distinction between absolute and conditional or hypothetical necessity. A necessity can be a merely hypothetical necessity even if the antecedent condition on which it is based is something which is eternally the case.

> Every contingent truth is necessary according to the disposition of the divine knowledge, even though many things are contingent between alternatives with respect to their secondary causes. For the following argument is valid: God wills this to be, or knows it will be; therefore, at the appropriate time it is the case. The antecedent is eternally true with respect to any past or future effect. So in relation to the foreknowledge of God every effect is necessary to come about. (U 333)

Aristotle had said that everything which is, when it is, necessarily is. We must make the same judgement, Wyclif says, about what will be and what has been. That is to say, what will be, will be necessary when it is. But is the future already necessary now?

> Once we have unravelled the ambiguity of 'necessity' it is clear how hypothetical necessity is consistent with supreme contingence. I do not mean sheerly hypothetical necessity, which does not posit either of the extremes, like 'If you are a donkey, you can be thwacked', because that is an absolutely necessary truth about the connection between the extremes. What I mean is an eternal contingent truth, entailing a truth occurring at a particular time, in such a way that the truth about the connection is absolutely necessary but the truth of the causal antecedent is contingent. (U 334)

What Wyclif means is this. We have the following valid argument:

(1) If God has always known that John will sin tomorrow, John will sin tomorrow.

(2) God has always known that John will sin tomorrow.

(3) Therefore, John will sin tomorrow.

The first proposition is absolutely necessary, an eternal truth about the relationship between the other two propositions. But the second proposition, though it is an eternal truth, that is to say a truth which has always been true, is not a necessary truth, but a contingent truth.

But how can there be contingent truths about God? Surely, if something is contingent it can cease to be the case and God is unchangeable. Wyclif has an answer to this:

> Although God can utterly contingently will or not will a given object of volition, he cannot begin or cease actually to will, and thus he cannot change from volition to non-volition or *vice versa*. (U 335)

God cannot change from knowing that *p* to knowing that not-*p*, or from willing *p* to be the case to not willing that *p* be the case; but when he knows that *p* is the case, sometimes (where *p* is a contingent truth) it would have been possible from all eternity that he knew that not-*p* was the case. If this seems difficult to grasp, Wyclif reminds us that even in human affairs it is often possible that *p*'s being the case is something that depends on a free action of mine, and yet there has never been a time when I can alter the truth-value of *p*. Thus, suppose it is true of me that I shall have a son. The coming true of this truth will depend, among other things, on free actions of mine. Yet at no time do I have the power to alter the truth value of the proposition 'I will have a son'. For if it is true of me now, it was true at the moment of my birth. Similarly, though the truth of any contingent truth in the universe depends, among other things, on God's volitions, there was no time at which God had the power to change those volitions or to alter the truth-values of the contingent truths.

The logical distinction between eternal contingent truths and necessary truths is well taken. But does the distinction avoid the problem of divine determinism? On Wyclif's own account, it is not possible for any secondary cause, like a human agent, to act except in so far as it is directed to do so by a first cause which is God. Does not this destroy freedom? In reply, Wyclif makes two points: no created cause can necessitate a free agent; and though God can necessitate a human agent, he cannot compel or constrain him.

> Although secondary causes can incline the created will to its proper act, neither they nor God can immediately compel it to the same, because, since the proper act of the will is willing, it is clear that it involves a contradiction that someone should perform such an act except willingly. However, God necessitates man to will good, and permits man to necessitate himself and subject himself to inferior creatures; and once withdrawn from God and enticed by the tempter, man will necessarily will evil. But the whole created universe, corporeal or spiritual, cannot drive a created will to that state unless it is willing.

Though sin diminishes liberty, it does not take it away altogether; and sin itself must have its origin in the sinner.

> It is possible for a child to walk freely, though necessitated to walk as he does by his tutor leading him by the hand; similarly it is possible for the created will to be led by the spirit of God. But man has the freedom to walk away from that saving guidance on the disobedient feet of pride. (U 340)

Wyclif's analogies are unconvincing, and it is hard to see how the distinction between necessitating and permitting is to apply in the case of an all-powerful God. The baby's steps are free simply because the nurse cannot make him walk, but only guide him where to go. Similarly, there is a distinction between what one human makes another do, and what he permits him to do; but this is only because human beings have an independence of each other which no creature has of God. If what I do is entailed by ideas and volitions in the mind of God, how can I have any real power to determine my own action? Wyclif puts the difficulty to himself very forcibly, in the following counter-argument to his thesis:

> It is necessary that particular events come about by absolute necessity, for God necessarily and independently fore-ordains, foresees, and wills, by the will of his good pleasure, every particular creature. Nothing can resist his will, and so nothing can prevent any effect. Just as no one can prevent the world's having been, no one can prevent any effect coming to be at the appropriate time. For the following argument is valid: God ordains this; therefore this will necessarily come to pass at the appropriate time. The antecedent is outside any created power and is accordingly altogether unpreventable. Similarly, therefore, is everything which formally follows from it. (U 342)

In the face of this objection, Wyclif reaffirms the crucial importance of human freedom: not just freedom from compulsion, but genuine freedom to choose between different alternatives.

Many effects are within rational creatures' free power

of choice between alternatives, in such a way that they can make them to be and make them not to be; otherwise merit and demerit would be eliminated. (U 343)

How are we to reconcile this with the divine control over human actions? Wyclif's proposed solution is that we should say that the relationship between the divine volition and the human action is a two-way one: if God's volition causes man's act, so, in a sense, man's act causes God's volition. It is in the power of man, with respect to many of God's eternal volitions, to bring about their non-existence, and similarly with his non-volitions and *vice versa*.

On this it is to be noted that the volition of God, with respect to the existence of a creature, can be understood as a relationship: a mental entity with its basis in God's willing the thing to be according to its mental being – which is something absolutely necessary – and with its terminus in the existence of the creature in its own kind. And such a relationship depends on each of the terms, since if God is to will that Peter or some other creature should be it is requisite that it should in fact be. And thus the existence of the creature, even though it is temporal, causes in God an eternal mental relationship, which is always in process of being caused and yet is always already completely caused. (U 343)

Thus, when God wills Peter to repent of his sin, it is true both that Peter is repenting because God wills him to repent, and that God wills him to repent because he is repenting (though this eternal volition of God's is a complex one which includes many other elements which are in no way dependent on Peter). So the objection that if

37

God's ordaining is outside our power, then all that follows from his ordaining is outside our power, is answered in a dramatic fashion. Wyclif simply denies the antecedent: God's ordaining is not altogether outside our power.

We can now see how wrong it is to suggest that Wyclif went beyond contemporary theologians in limiting human freedom in the interests of divine omnipotence. On the contrary, he took the highly unusual step of safeguarding human freedom by attributing to it control over the eternal volitions of God himself.

It cannot be claimed that Wyclif's solution resolves the problem of freedom and foreknowledge. Any objector will simply wish to rephrase his objection in terms of the absolute mental volitions instead of the complex relational ones. But no other medieval theologian succeeded in giving a satisfactory answer to the antinomy, and perhaps no satisfactory answer will ever be possible. Where Wyclif departs from his colleagues is not in imputing extra necessity to human actions, but in assigning unusual contingency to divine volitions. If others deny such contingent volitions, he tells us, that is simply because of their ignorance of metaphysics.

Wyclif's solution to the antinomy may seem to involve the absurdity of causation which operates backwards in time. That is not necessarily so, given his doctrine that all things are present with God. Summing up his treatment of divine foreknowledge of contingent events he says:

> All these and similar things are obvious from the infallible principle that with God all things which have ever been or will be are present, and thus, if something has been or will be, it is at the appropriate time. Blessed, then, be the Lord of time, who has lifted us above time to see that resplendent truth and all the other things that

follow from it. For this is the key to the doctrines of predestination and foreknowledge and the entire topic of the necessity of future contingents. (U 347)

When Wyclif says that all things are present to God, he does not simply mean that God now knows the events of all times and thus has them all present in his mind. This is something which few medieval theologians would have denied. He means to offer the presentiality of things as some kind of an account of *how* God knows them. Presentiality in this sense would have been denied by many theologians: God cannot know the future *as* present, since it isn't present; he knows the future in its present causes here and now. But in affirming that all things are present to God, Wyclif is following in the footsteps of highly orthodox theologians such as Aquinas who have never been accused of being determinists. And when Wyclif differs from Aquinas in this matter, he diverges in the direction of contingence, rather than necessity, since he regarded the decrees of God as contingent, whereas Aquinas treats them as necessary.

There is no doubt that Wyclif believed in predestination, that is to say, he believed that no one could be saved who had not been predestined to salvation by God. But this belief was in no way a peculiar feature of his theological system: it was a belief shared by all those who accepted the authority of St Augustine. When, at the Reformation, predestination became an issue of discord between Catholics and Protestants, what was in question was not whether those who were saved were predestined by God: that was accepted by both sides. The disagreement was whether those who were damned were also predestined to be damned, as some of the Reformers insisted. This doctrine has seemed to many people to be a corollary of the

39

doctrine of the predestination of the saved, given a theoretical framework in which the only final alternatives are salvation and damnation. But predestination to damnation was denied by Catholics at the Reformation, and had been denied in official Church documents since the Council of Orange in 529. That Council, having affirmed in Augustinian terms the impotence of human beings to be saved without unearned, prevenient grace, went on to say 'but as for some people being predestined to evil by divine power, this we not only do not believe, but if there are any who would believe something so wicked, we pronounce an anathema upon them'.

According to Catholic doctrine, while the elect were predestined to heaven, the damned were only foreknown as hell-bound. God's knowledge was equal in the two cases; but the attitude of his will was not equal. God knew that certain people would be damned with the same certainty as he knew that others would be saved; but the career of the elect was dependent on a decree of his will in a way in which the career of the damned was not. The language we have just seen in Wyclif accords with this: God necessitates to good willing, but only permits man to be enticed to evil.

Whether in the case of God the distinction between foreordaining and foreknowing can be consistently maintained, or the distinction between necessitation and permission, is something which is not easy to determine. But there is no doubt that Wyclif made and emphasized the distinction in his philosophical works; and in doing so he was at one with the Catholic tradition. This was not something which he abandoned in the course of his quarrel with the Church. When, towards the end of his life, he raises in ever more strident tones the question whether the Pope and prelates are among those who are predestined to bliss, the word he uses as the alternative is always '*praescitus*' or 'foreknown'. Even when he wishes to portray them most vigorously as hell-bound, he never suggests that they are predestined to damnation. Throughout his life he continued to draw the distinctions which enabled him to maintain simultaneously the necessity of all that happens and the freedom of human agency and sin. His critics would have done well to attend to the remark in *On Universals* with which he concludes his treatment of the topic:

> No one should casually speak simply of contingent and necessary; by making distinctions I reconcile opinions which seem verbally to be contrary to each other. (U 166)

4 Grace and dominion

While writing his philosophical works, Wyclif continued to live, for the most part, in Oxford; he supported himself from the revenues of a succession of benefices in various parts of the country. The Mastership of Balliol was no great prize, and he quickly abandoned it for the college living of Fillingham in 1361. A year later the University petitioned Urban V (the sixth and penultimate Avignon Pope) to make him in addition a canon of York; he was awarded instead a prebend in Westbury church near Bristol. He was dispensed from residence in his benefices in order to study for his doctorate of divinity, and from 1363 he rented rooms in Queen's College. We do not know whether he was any more careful than other absentee pluralists to ensure that his duties were well carried out in his absence. But his surviving works show that he was assiduous in his Oxford studies, and in 1365 he was appointed to the headship of a new and experimental Oxford college, Canterbury Hall. Archbishop Islip of Canterbury had founded a mixed institution for monks and seculars, designed no doubt in an ecumenical spirit as a focus of harmony between these constantly quarrelling groups. The experiment failed almost as soon as it began; when Wyclif became the hall's second warden the monastic fellows were expelled, and when the monks secured their reinstatement Wyclif himself was deposed. He appealed to Urban V against this deposition, but lost his appeal and was soon back in his rooms in Queen's. In the mean time, in 1368, he exchanged the rectory of Fillingham for the less prosperous, but more convenient, living of Ludgershall in Buckinghamshire. He was clearly no stranger to the benefice-hunting characteristic of the age; and when, in 1371, Pope Gregory XI made him a canon of Lincoln and promised him the next vacant prebend there, he seemed to have his feet firmly set on the ladder of ecclesiastical promotion.

Meanwhile, he was acquiring a reputation as a theologian. His first purely theological work, *On the Incarnation of the Word*, was written as a commentary on the *Sentences* of Peter Lombard, the standard lecture-text in theology. The treatise, which is orthodox and unremarkable, occupies in Wyclif's theological career the place of a doctoral dissertation in the modern curriculum. Having completed it, he took his DD in 1372. He soon set himself to compose a theological *summa* to match his philosophical *summa*. It was to be his major life's work, he announced in the treatise *On Divine Dominion*, begun in 1373 as a prolegomenon to the encyclopaedic work which he projected. The *summa* was indeed brought to completion, eight years later; but by then it had turned into something totally different from a typical schoolman's exposition of his theological system. Even the writing of the preliminary *On Divine Dominion* was interrupted before the book was half complete. Wyclif was invited to enter the royal service.

The invitation offered an opportunity to help settle a long-festering dispute between Church and State, between the King's Council and the Curia of the Popes at Avignon. The Popes had long claimed, and from time to time exercised, the right to tax the English clergy, and the right to appoint, or 'provide', to senior posts in the English Church. Bishops and abbots, and clergy who held endowed positions in cathedrals and large churches, could draw substantial incomes from these benefices; but to be appointed they needed Papal provision, for which they must pay a fat fee to Avignon, and sometimes the whole revenue of the first year of incumbency, known as 'annates'. In addition, clerical incomes were sometimes taxed; but English kings did not always permit their clergy to honour the claims thus made on them, and when they did, it was often in return for a substantial percentage of the takings. During the first part of the Hundred Years' War the Papal taxes were not collected: English monarchs felt that enough English gold went to the French Pope in Avignon in the form of annates, and they preferred to tax their clergy for their own war effort.

The Statute of Provisors in 1351 and the Statute of Praemunire in 1353 outlawed Papal presentations to benefices in England: to procure them, or to appeal to the Pope's courts in connection with them, became a crime. The law, however, was hardly ever put into operation, and Papal provision went on as before, as Wyclif's own career illustrates. In 1373 it was decided to try to negotiate an agreement with the Pope about taxation, provision, and appeals. The issue of taxation had come to a head because, just after a Parliament in 1371 had forced on the reluctant clergy a levy of £50,000 to pay for the English wars in France, Gregory XI made a claim for £20,000 to finance a war in Italy by which he hoped to recover the Papal dominions.

Wyclif attended the Parliament of 1371, and listened to two friars speak in support of the Government's right not only to tax but actually to confiscate church property for public purposes. Three deputations were sent across the channel to negotiate with the Papal officers about provision and taxation, and Wyclif was invited to take part in the second delegation. Though he was the second in command in the party, he seems to have had little influence on the course of the talks. This was as well for his reputation, since the eventual outcome was regarded as a defeat for the royal negotiators: Pope Gregory reserved his right to make provisions, and his tax was to be paid, though only in instalments. But Wyclif's involvement in the dispute determined the turn of his theological researches for the next few years.

The first two books of Wyclif's theological *summa*, *On the Divine Commandments* and *On the State of Innocence*, had been discreet and orthodox works with no particular topical relevance: an exposition of the ten commandments, heavily indebted to Grosseteste, and a brief speculative tract on the nature of human life before the fall of Adam. But the third treatise, *On Civil Dominion*, a massive work in three books, is a systematic and radical examination of the issues which had preoccupied the parliament of 1371 and the negotiators at Bruges.

The first book announces two resounding theses: a man in sin has no right to dominion or lordship; a man who is in a state of grace possesses all the goods of the universe.

The first thesis is argued for thus. You cannot justly possess a thing unless you can justly use it. But if a man is in a state of sin, every one of his actions is unjust; he cannot, therefore, use anything justly, and consequently cannot possess anything justly. All lordship must be granted by God; but God makes no grant to those who are in enmity with him. Of course he gives them whatever they have, in the sense that he allows them to make use of it all; but he does not make any grant of goods that would confer a right to them.

There are three kinds of possession: natural, civil, and evangelical. Suppose Peter occupies by force the territory which Paul has inherited. Peter has nothing but natural possession, whereas Paul has civil possession. But it is only if Paul is in a state of grace that Paul has evangelical possession. No human being can confer title to property: human witnesses merely give evidence, and human judges must act as God's instruments. Human inheritance can be forfeited by disloyalty to one's civil lord; how much more then does forfeiture follow sin which is treason against the Lord of All!

> If I lend you my horse on certain conditions and for a certain term, and you without licence go beyond the contract and its terms, your possession of my horse is surely unjust. Similarly, God stipulates with his servants for continual service, sets terms to use, and forbids abuse; there is no doubt then that whoever abuses his power is in unjust possession of the goods of God without licence, and therefore the Almighty by that very fact deprives him of his right. (W 1885. 45)

The just man, on the other hand, possesses justly not only those things to which he has a civil right, but the whole visible world. He is the adoptive son of God, and so is lord of God's realm. When God gives grace, he gives himself and all that is in himself: and in him is the ideal reality of all creatures, to which their actual existence can be viewed as a mere accessory. As Adam, before his fall, was lord of the visible universe, so too is the redeemed Christian in a state of grace; indeed in several ways his lordship is even more ample. Wyclif goes through the various categories of goods – chattels, reputation, friendship, property, authority – and offers to prove of each of them in turn that they cannot be possessed without grace, and must be possessed with grace.

But if each Christian has lordship over all, it can only be on condition that he shares his lordship with all others who are likewise in a state of grace. Thus Wyclif proves that goods ought to be held in common:

All the goods of God should be common. This is proved thus. Every man should be in a state of grace; and if he is in a state of grace, he is lord of the world and all it contains. So every man should be lord of the universe. But this is not consistent with there being many men, unless they ought to have everything in common. Therefore all things should be in common. (W 1885. 96)

This argument, he says, should bring conviction to any Catholic; but he takes time to argue against Aristotle's criticisms of the communism propounded in Plato's *Republic*. There is no need to carry things as far as Plato does, and commend wife-sharing; but in essence the Platonic theory is sound. Civil property becomes theft when its owners sin: the rich who abuse their temporal goods do the poor an injustice, since the goods they are squandering belong to the poor. The theory of communism is biblical as well as Platonic: did not St Paul say to the Corinthians 'All things are yours'?

In the second section of Book One, *On Civil Dominion* discusses the relationship between divine and human law. Divine law is the perfect law given by Christ, the Old and New Testament for the ruling of the Catholic Church. How can any human law then be necessary? If it is implicit in the Gospel law it will therefore be superfluous. If it is contrary to it, it will be wicked. If it claims to be additional to it, it will be impudently imputing insufficiency to the perfect law of God. Much in human law is indeed vain and hurtful; but the parts of it which are in accord with Gospel law can be regarded as different clothings of the same reality. Human law is commonly divided into canon law, regulating the clerical part of the Church, and civil law, regulating the lay part of the Church. But this division is a seed-bed of great discord in the holy Church of God.

47

It cannot be said that Wyclif teases out the relationships between these different laws in a way which would provide usable criteria for resolving conflicts between them; but he carries on a lively polemic against a number of alleged principles of human law which he regards as diabolically corrupt: as, for instance, the thesis that the best of all titles is the right of conquest.

In the third part of the book nine chapters are devoted to the classical question of medieval political theorists: how is the state best governed? He presents a case for kingship, and a case for aristocracy, and concludes, as did most theorists living in monarchies, that it is best for men, the sinful world being what it is, to be under the government of kings. But what if the kings are tyrants? Even so, they should be obeyed, as Christ obeyed Herod and Pilate; they should have taxes paid to them, as Christ paid tax to Caesar. However, if the refusal to pay would be likely to bring to an end the tyrannical misrule, then the subject may legitimately withdraw his support (W 1885. 201).

Should monarchy be hereditary or elective? There are advantages on both sides; but neither succession nor election by itself confers title without grace. The theologian should not take sides on the issue: the matter must be left to God, Lord in chief and Father of all, who ever since the time of Cain has often overturned the order of primogeniture.

From monarchy Wyclif turns to slavery: is it lawful for Christians to have slaves?

By the law of Christ every man is bound to love his neighbour as himself; but every slave is a neighbour of every civil lord; therefore every civil lord must love any of his slaves as himself; but by natural instinct every lord abhors slavery; therefore by the law of charity he is bound not to impose slavery on any brother in Christ.

After this resplendent application of the golden rule, however, Wyclif goes on to allow that even hereditary slavery may be permissible in very special circumstances (W 1885. 227).

So far, the treatise has operated at a highly abstract level. It is not easy to see what practical conclusions are to be drawn from the considerations of lordship, government, and property. If the legitimacy of any claim made upon us by a landlord or governor depends upon his being in a state of grace, it is clearly important that we should be able to recognize such a state when we see it. But how are we to know who has God's grace? How can we tell who is predestined to eternal happiness in heaven?

Wyclif is exasperatingly reluctant to spell out this obvious difficulty and to offer an answer to it. If we are charitably to give everyone the benefit of the doubt, and assume that they are in a state of grace, then the practical consequences of the theory of dominion will be nil. Some of the claims made on us will be unjustified; but we should honour them since, for all we know, the claimant has a justified title. But this does not seem to be Wyclif's view. Some people, he believes, are such manifest sinners, that we are justified in rejecting their titles as of now. And such manifest sinners, it transpires, are particularly to be found in the ranks of the clergy.

The final section of the book is devoted to this burning question of the circumstances in which priests and prelates forfeit their right to church property.

> From all this it follows that whenever an ecclesiastical community or person habitually abuses its wealth, kings, princes and temporal lords can take it away,

however much it may be established by human tradition. (W 1885. 266)

It does not matter if secular rulers who confiscate church property are excommunicated for doing so. No one can be excommunicated unless he excommunicates himself: it is sin which places a man outside the communion of the faithful, and a priest can do no more than publish this fact. Taxation cannot be enforced by excommunication, and gifts to the clergy must be voluntary. Not even the Pope is justified in excommunicating for the sake of money, and any attempt to exercise such a power is null.

But what of Christ's promise to Peter and to his successors, 'Whatever thou shalt bind on earth shall be bound in heaven, and whatever thou shalt loose on earth shall be loosed in heaven'? This text, Wyclif says, misunderstood, puts fear into many simple Christians. It was a contract which God made with Peter, the captain of the apostles, whereby he promised to him and the priests his successors that he would give them the keys of the kingdom of heaven. If they used their powers unerringly, he would graciously be present to effectuate their sentence. This is one of the greatest privileges ever conferred on a mortal.

But to avoid heresy it must be noted that it is not possible that if the Pope or anyone else by some symbol or other claims to bind or loose, the binding and loosing automatically takes place. If you grant this you have to grant that the Pope cannot sin, and therefore that he is God; otherwise he could go wrong and act out of conformity with the key of Christ . . . It is impossible for any vicar or prelate of Christ to open or close, unless he acts in conformity with the key of Christ which has already opened or closed; otherwise he would be another God in opposition to our God. (W 1885. 283)

Not only endowments may be removed from clergy who abuse the incomes therefrom: the tithes too paid to churchmen can be withheld when the holder of a benefice fails to carry out the duties of his cure. The payment of tithes is indeed obligatory in the New Testament as in the Old; but the purpose of this obligation is to enable the clergy to succour the poor; so if they fail in this duty, tithes can be paid directly to the poor, or through lay almoners (W 1885. 340).

> From all this it appears that in a possible emergency the church of England can legitimately and meritoriously take away from the clergy the goods of the poor from religious houses, if it be the case that they are squandering them prodigally on themselves and their friends, stubbornly witholding them from the poor, and being distracted by them from their religious purpose to worldly dominion along with layfolk. (W 1885. 345)

It would be a calumny against the laws of England to deny that the King may confiscate property from delinquent clergy.

But are not kings and all layfolk bound to obey the Church with the same reverence as they obey the Gospel? The Church, which is the bride and body of Christ, is the totality of those who are predestinate, whether dead, or alive or yet to be born. No particular church can claim the reverence due to this. A Pope may sin as Peter sinned; he can err in matters of morals as of doctrine. Neither Pope nor cardinals are essential to the government of the Church; for if a Pope is not one of the predestinate he is not part of the Church, and yet the Church remains. Wyclif does not deny, but reaffirms that the Pope's rule is to be obeyed by Christians, and treated as apostolical command. But the Pope is to be obeyed only in so far as he obeys the Church, and the Church's head, by basing his judgement on scripture.

> But it could happen that he and his friends should be so intent on worldly matters that they should believe the church would be brought to an end if they lacked temporal lordship; they might be so mad as to think that nothing in a particular church was lawful unless it came from and was authenticated by their own court, and that any letters sent from the Pope are to obeyed with a like obedience to the Gospel; they might fall into many absurd blasphemies, and fall away from the religion of Christ and pave the way for the blasphemy of Antichrist. I do not assert that this is how things are; I merely say that it is a possibility. And if it came to pass, every Christian should resist until the clothes are torn off his back and his limbs are mangled. (W 1885. 384)

The second and third books of the *On Civil Dominion* add little new to the contents of the first: they are, indeed, a defence of the earlier volume in answer to an Oxford cleric who had attacked the first instalment. They make in greater detail the case for despoiling delinquent clergy, with copious allusions to historical precedents. The first book of the work, indeed, contains in germ many of the characteristic doctrines which Wyclif was later to develop at greater length: the sufficiency of scripture, the Church of the predestinate, and the ambiguous nature of Papal power, capable of spreading either the gospel of Christ or the blasphemies of Antichrist.

The publication of *On Civil Dominion* drew favourable notice from powerful lay nobles in England and hostile attention from the English bishops and the Papal court at Avignon. John of Gaunt, anxious to assert his authority against clerical statesmen like Bishop Wykeham of

Winchester and Bishop Courtenay of London, summoned Wyclif to London and encouraged him to preach a series of sermons denouncing the bishops' worldliness and wealth. Courtenay, a high-born, strong-willed prelate with powerful connections, summoned Wyclif to face an ecclesiastical tribunal in St Paul's. Wyclif appeared, accompanied not only by four advocates from the religious orders who shared his animus against clerical riches, but also by John of Gaunt and his ally Lord Percy, the Marshal of England. For the present he was safe with such powerful defenders, and the trial got no further than an exchange of insults between the noblemen and the prelate. Londoners demonstrated and rioted in defence of their bishop against the threats of Gaunt and Percy, and Wyclif slipped away to Oxford.

This was in February 1377. At about the same time, someone was drawing the anti-clerical contents of *On Civil Dominion* to the attention of the Papal court. In May Pope Gregory picked out eighteen propositions from the work, and sent bulls in condemnation of them to the King, to the senior bishops, and to the University of Oxford. The bishops were to discover whether these theses were indeed taught by Wyclif: if so, they were to gaol him to get a confession to send to Avignon. If they were unable to do so, Wyclif was to be cited to appear himself before the Papal court. The university was to eradicate the evil doctrines, and hand over Wyclif and his disciples to the bishops.

These bulls were never put into effect. Edward III died in June and his bull had to be readdressed to the new King, Richard II. Wyclif was not put in gaol; he agreed to a nominal house-arrest in an Oxford hall. The chancellor of the University, having consulted his colleagues, said that the condemned theses 'though they sounded ill to the ear, were none the less true'.

The royal council, so far from attemping to enforce Gregory's bull, employed Wyclif as an official consultant. He was asked to opine 'whether the kingdom of England may lawfully, in case of necessity, for its own defence, detain and keep back the treasure of the kingdom' even if the Pope himself demanded it under threat. Not surprisingly, the minute of advice which he wrote in reply gave the desired affirmative answer.

Even the bishops did not press the charges against Wyclif. In March 1378, four months after the bulls' publication, they summoned him to trial at Lambeth; but they were warned by the Queen mother that any drastic proceedings against him would be ill received. So they contented themselves with forbidding him to maintain his theses in lectures or in sermons, lest scandal be given to the laity. Wyclif observed that to condemn a truth 'because it sounds bad to sinners and fools' would 'make all Scripture liable to condemnation'.

He was still at liberty when death took off the Pope who had sought to condemn him. Gregory, at the end of his life, had brought the Papacy back to Rome from Avignon; the last of the French line of Popes, he was succeeded by an Italian, Urban VI, learned, austere, and bent on reform. Wyclif welcomed the election, and wrote to the new Pope to excuse himself from answering his predecessor's citation to Rome.

I am glad to declare to any man the faith I hold, and especially to the bishop of Rome; for I suppose that if it is orthodox he will humbly confirm it, and if it is in error he will amend it. But I suppose that the gospel of Christ is the body of God's law . . . and that the bishop of Rome, as the supreme vicar of Christ on earth, is the most bound of all pilgrims to that law of the gospel . . .

Christ, during the time of his pilgrimage here was a most poor man, who cast off all worldly dominion . . . From this I gather, that ideally the Pope should leave all temporal dominion to the secular power, and should effectually urge his clergy to do likewise . . . But if I have erred in this I am humbly ready to make amends, if necessary by death. (W 1910. 1)

Wyclif ended his letter with a prayer that God 'will so stir up our pope Urban VI as he began that he with his clergy may follow the Lord Jesus Christ in life and manners'.

Wyclif was not alone in hoping for great things from the new Pope. But within a few months all such hopes were dashed: there broke out a great schism which was to bring more evil into the Church than even the Avignon exile had done.

5 The truth of scripture

Pope Urban's reforming zeal soon turned into paranoid bullying. He alienated the cardinals who had elected him, and they began to claim they had chosen him under duress, to satisfy the clamours of the Roman mob for an Italian Pope. In September 1378 they held a second conclave and elected as Pope Robert of Geneva, who took the name of Clement VII. The new Pope was best known as the bloodthirsty commander of the war against Florence for which Pope Gregory had been so eager to tax England. Clement moved back to Avignon, taking the cardinals with him. Urban had to create a complete new college; even of these, six proved unfaithful, and the new Pope had them tortured by a Genoese pirate and thrown into the sea. For nearly forty years there were two Popes, one at Rome and one at Avignon; attempts to reunite the Papacy only succeeded in producing a third would-be Pope. It was not until 1417, long after Wyclif's death, that Europe was again united in allegiance to a single Pope. England supported the Roman line, and France the Avignon line; throughout Europe men debated which was the rightful claimant to the See of Peter. Macaulay has well described this melancholy schism.

> Two Popes, each with a doubtful title, made all Europe ring with their mutual invectives and anathemas. Rome cried out against the corruptions of Avignon; and Avignon, with equal justice, recriminated on Rome. The plain Christian people, brought up in the belief that it was a sacred duty to be in communion with the head of

56

the Church, were unable to discover, amidst conflicting testimonies and conflicting arguments, to which of the two worthless priests who were cursing and reviling each other the headship of the Church rightfully belonged.

It was probably the schism which saved Wyclif from further Papal prosecution. Urban VI was too preoccupied with his troubles in Rome to follow up the abortive bulls of Gregory XI, and was in any case wary of doing anything to disturb the precarious allegiance of England. No anathema was placed on Wyclif by the universal Church until long after his death. Then, the Council of Constance, which put an end to the schism, made the condemnation of Wycliffite heresies its other major item of business. But while the schism shielded Wyclif from Papal attack, it also hastened his disillusionment with the Papacy as an institution. For centuries the Papal office, despite the faults of its holders, had served as a focus for the unity of Christendom; but after 1378 the rival Popes of the schism, far from being symbols of concord, were active fomentors of discord.

When the schism broke out, Wyclif was working on one of the most substantial treatises of his theological *summa*, entitled *On the Truth of Sacred Scripture*. The work is a defence of the authority and inerrancy of the Bible; one of the writings which earned Wyclif the soubriquet 'Evangelical Doctor'. The tone is often polemical, and Wyclif writes as if he were surrounded by people who accuse the Bible of containing absurd errors, and who rate its authority much below that of pagan philosophers or Papal decretals. It is difficult to know how far he is attacking real opponents and how far he is setting up men of straw; but the treatise is a systematic, if digressive, treatise on the problems of scriptural interpretation which will bear comparison with anything similar in the Latin Middle Ages.

When he came to write the treatise, Wyclif had already had a long practical experience of Bible study. During the years 1371 and 1376 he probably lectured regularly on scripture texts; and he distilled his lectures into a line-by-line commentary on each of the books. This commentary was long believed lost, but in fact it had been preserved in manuscripts in various libraries in England and Bohemia. In 1953 the discovery, under ultra-violet light, of an expunged attribution to Wyclif in a Bodleian manuscript Bible commentary enabled the whole scattered corpus to be pieced together. Though the commentary is largely a catena of quotations from previous commentators, and though it leans heavily on the work of a Parisian exegete, Nicholas of Lyra, it is a massive enterprise which had no parallel among English academics for several centuries before and after. It gave Wyclif an unrivalled knowledge of the biblical text and of the interpretations offered of each passage by the Church Fathers.

Wyclif's work on the Bible kept him at Oxford, and he cannot have spent much time with his parishioners. In *On the Truth of Sacred Scripture* he interrupts a denunciation of absentee clergy with a passage pointing out that there may be occasions when absence is justified.

It is lawful for a rector for a time to gather the seed of faith in theological schools away from his parish, with a view to sowing it at an opportune time. Spiritual food is more effective and permanent than bodily food, so it is enough if a pastor feeds his charges at appropriate times in the year, provided that he profits them continually by his priestly life and trains a suitable substitute. (W 1907. 39)

We must assume at these appropriate times he visited his parishioners; meanwhile, he proceeded with his treatise on the Bible.

Wyclif has three principal aims in the treatise. First, he wishes to show that the Bible is free from error, and has authority derived from its divine authorship. Secondly, he claims that all truth is in the Bible, and that the Bible text must be the yardstick to judge the innovations of Popes, theologians, lawyers, and philosophers. Thirdly, since the Bible contains the whole truth and nothing but the truth, it must be placed at the disposal of all Christians, priests and laymen alike.

First, then, the Bible is true and authoritative. If, in places, it contradicts Aristotle, so much the worse for Aristotle; nobody, even young students studying philosophy, should ever deny that the world was created out of nothing, or call in question any other article of faith. The Bible has its own logic; an eternal logic, free from the vagaries of human fashion; so unlike the logics taught at Oxford where a logical system never lasts as long as twenty years. Despite appearances, the Bible is free from internal contradiction; it can always be given a consistent sense if an interpreter will examine the texts carefully, compare the different parts of the sacred books with each other, and above all seek divine illumination in prayer. Wyclif devotes considerable energy to discussing a number of familiar cruces in which the inspired authors seem to contradict each other. He explains in what way we are to understand texts that are, in their literal sense, false: allegories, parables, and fictions of other kinds.

The authority of scripture is greater than the capacity of

the human mind; hence, if you think you find error in the Bible, that shows that there is something wrong with your interpretation. If a Christian thinks he finds falsehood in scripture, that is a falsehood which he has put there himself; the real sense of the text must be something other than the one he attributes to it.

In attributing inerrancy to the Bible in this way Wyclif was merely following Catholic tradition. He himself quotes a passage from Thomas Aquinas:

> It is not lawful to believe that there are any false assertions in the gospel or in any canonical writing; nor can one say that the writers uttered any falsehood in them; that would mean that there would be an end of the certainty of faith, which rests on the authority of sacred scripture.

It is wrong to think of Wyclif as a fundamentalist, clinging to every jot and tittle of a sacred text. The scripture of which he speaks with such veneration is something more complicated than a Bible on a bookshelf.

> It has been my custom to list five degrees of sacred scripture. The first is the book of life mentioned in Apocalypse 20 and 21. The second is the truths written in the book of life in their ideal being . . . In the third sense Scripture means the truths which are to be believed in general, which, in their existence or effect, are written in the book of life. In the fourth sense Scripture means a truth to be believed as it is written in the natural book which is a man's soul . . . In the fifth sense Scripture means the books or sounds or other artificial signs of truth. (W 1905. 109)

There may, then, be a contradiction in the written Bible which is not a contradiction in the real sacred scripture.

'For sacred scripture is the combination of the written book, and the sacred sense or meaning which a Catholic derives from the material text which is its symbol.' The mental understanding of the text is more truly the holy scripture than are the lines on the paper. What is on the paper is not scripture without its relation to the mental understanding; and what is in the mind is not holy unless it is a grasping of the objective scripture. Hence the need to compare manuscripts together, and check them against the common faith of the whole Church (W 1905. 189).

Wyclif raises the question of the canon or definition of scripture. We may agree that the books of scripture have authority, but how do we know which books count as scripture? Wyclif argues for the authenticity of various books of the Old Testament on the grounds of their being quoted in the New; but he does not altogether avoid the circularity which threatens anyone who tries to determine the canon of scripture on the basis of scripture alone. He discusses the status of apocryphal books such as the gospel of Nicodemus, but dismisses them in a rather cavalier manner. We have twenty-two books in the Old Testament, and twenty-four in the new; we can soldier on with these, and to canonize any more would be burdensome. Written texts are, after all, only beasts of burden to carry the sacred message.

Thus far, Wyclif's book can be seen to be an early example of the kind of defence which might be offered by a nineteenth-century apologist against the inroads of biblical criticism. But there is another strand in his thought which resembles rather the writings of sixteenth-century reformers who insisted that all truth is to be found in the Bible, and that there is no independent access to divine revelation through unwritten tradition handed down in the Church. This is, however, less strongly emphasized in this work than when Wyclif later came to deal expressly with the Papal claims. But the work frequently repeats that scripture contains all truth, and in one passage Wyclif even offers to prove his own atomic theory out of it, from the beginning of Genesis and from Matthew 10:30. He sums up:

> An argument drawn from the faith of scripture is the most powerful and certain of all . . . For since the whole of sacred scripture is the word of God, there could not be a superior, safer, or more effective testimony than this: if God who cannot lie says this in his scripture, which is the mirror of his will, then it is true. (W 1905. 378)

Just as all rivers run to the sea, so all created authority must in the end rest on the uncreated authority of God. Even such things as the veracity of maxims of reasoning, the validity of syllogistic form, the reliability of human testimony or inductive evidence – all these depend for their credibility on the word of God.

> The reason that they are true and worthy of belief is that God says them. For since God says all truth it is clear that his saying is the first cause of all truth outside himself.

The Koran of Mahomet and the Decretals of the Popes have distracted attention from the incomparable pre-eminence of the Bible. This is a sign of the approach of Antichrist, and the only remedy for modern superstition is

> to believe solidly in the faith of scripture, and to believe no one else on any topic except to the extent to which he bases himself on scripture. (W 1905. 382)

The ecclesiastical authorities may not contradict, nor add to scripture; they may only interpret it. But they do not have a monopoly of its correct interpretation.

> Even the lord Pope, or any other grandee, may be ignorant of the sense of Scripture and in a greedy quest for wealth interpret it in a sense contrary to Christ. But since every error which is corrigible can be amended by a return to first principles, it seems that there is a logic of supreme correctness which must be regarded as a foundation, and that is nothing but the form of the words of Scripture. (W 1905. 384)

So everyone must become a theologian, and the scripture be given to all.

> Some worldly folk puffed up with learning treat Scripture lightly and irreverently, despising its logic and style; they are like the gentiles who thought Christ a fool for his humility and patience. But the faithful whom he calls in meekness and humility of heart, whether they be clergy or laity, male or female, bending the neck of their inner man to the logic and style of Scripture will find in it the power to labour and the wisdom hidden from the proud. (W 1905. 117)

On the Truth of Sacred Scripture ranges over more topics than its title immediately suggests. A long section is devoted to the question how far the ceremonial laws of the Old Testament are obligatory in the New: must a Christian, for instance, eat only kosher meat? Nearly a hundred pages, including some of the most carefully argued portions of the book, are devoted to the question whether lying is always wrong, or whether a Christian may sometimes tell lies in a good cause. Wyclif takes the strict line that nothing whatever can ever justify a falsehood. The discussion wanders far from the exegesis of scripture, but its connection with the main topic is clear: if lying is not always morally wrong, then one cannot argue from God's supreme goodness to prove that whatever is contained in his word must be true. If lying were ever justified, then

> Christ might have been telling lies all through his Scripture about the everlasting punishment of sin, telling this to his church only to put fear into it. It is within the bounds of the absolute power of God to save all men, even on the supposition of their committing all the sins they have now committed. In the same way Christ might have uttered all the things he said about perpetual punishment merely as a threat . . . The strongest evidence [for eternal punishment] is the evidence of Scripture; but with respect to all the texts which might be quoted, it could plausibly be said that they are pious lies to deter men from committing evils.

The impossible and heretical nature of the idea that all rational creatures might be saved is enough to show us the folly of the underlying thesis that lying may sometimes be justified. Wyclif puts the poisonous thought away with a shudder (W 1906. 54).

So the laity as well as the clergy are to familiarize themselves with the whole of the Bible, and not just the passages suggested for Sunday and feast day readings. Does this mean that every farm-hand will have to learn Latin? Wyclif does not address the question in *On the Truth of Sacred Scripture*; but a small work of uncertain date, the *Mirror of Secular Lords*, begins by stating that the truths of the faith and the demands of the law of Christ must be set out in the vernacular as well as in Latin.

Christ and his apostles converted a great multitude by

unveiling sacred scripture to them, and that in the language which was most familiar to the people. That was why the Holy Spirit gave them the knowledge of all tongues. Why then should not modern disciples of Christ [do likewise]? . . . The faith of Christ must be unlocked to the people in each of the languages of which the Holy Spirit has given us knowledge. (W 1910. 75)

And in a polemical work, written towards the end of his life, he says:

The language of a book, whether Hebrew, Greek, Latin or English, is the vesture of the law of God. And in whatever clothing its message is most truly understood by the faithful, in that is the book most reasonably to be accepted. For mere language, whether on earth or in heaven, is remote from the message and law of God, since the division of tongues was introduced by God and the devil as a punishment for the sin of pride of the builders of the tower of Babel. (W 1883. 701)

Did Wyclif himself begin this task of clothing the word of God in the new vesture of English? He does not claim the honour in any of his surviving works; but then he is not in general very communicative about himself, except to defend himself from accusations of heresy, or occasionally to admit to faults such as youthful arrogance in debate, or over-eating at common table (W 1905. 363). The early manuscripts of the English Bible do not bear Wyclif's name but a chronicler writing in 1390 says that in 1382 he translated the gospel into English, so that what was formerly the exclusive possession of the learned clergy 'was made available to any lay person, even woman, who knew how to read'. Most scholars nowadays seem unconvinced that the two versions of the English Bible which have come down to us from this period were written, or even supervised, by Wyclif himself. But they were undoubtedly the work of men influenced and inspired by his teaching. One version, a very literal and Latinate one, is commonly attributed to Nicholas of Hereford, the leader of the Wycliffite party at Oxford in the early 1380s after Wyclif himself had left the University. The other version, in more natural English, is commonly associated, rightly or wrongly, with John Purvey, who was the reformer's companion and perhaps secretary during the last years of his life, when he retired to Lutterworth.

Over two hundred manuscripts of the versions survive; this despite the fact that during the persecution of Wyclif's followers after his death possession of them was made illegal and taken as evidence of heretical leanings. In fact, the translation, though containing the proportion of errors to be expected in the execution of such a novel and gigantic task, is not at all tendentious. Unlike some Reformation versions it does not attempt to make controversial capital by its choice of terms to correspond to Latin words which had become associated with Catholic dogmas. Here, for instance, in modernized spelling, is the text of Christ's promise to Peter that was taken by the Popes as the charter of their power (Matthew 16:18–19).

I say to thee, for thou art Peter, and upon this stone I shall build my church, and the gates of hell shall not have might against it. And to thee I shall give the keys of the kingdom of heaven; and what ever thou shalt bind upon earth shall be bounden and in heavens; and what ever thou shalt unbind upon earth, shall be unbounden and in heavens.

No Catholic could take exception on doctrinal grounds to any of the translation here.

Whatever part Wyclif may have had in it, the translation of the Bible was some years in the future at the time of the writing of *On the Truth of Sacred Scripture*, which was completed about the end of 1378. Wyclif's career of service to the government had not yet quite come to an end. In 1377 a prisoner who had escaped from the Tower of London and taken refuge in Westminster Abbey had been killed by royal officers along with a sacristan. Those responsible for the killing were excommunicated by the Archbishop of Canterbury; the royal Council in reply summoned the Abbot of Westminster to appear before Parliament. To avoid local prejudice the Parliament was held in Gloucester; and Wyclif was invited to plead before it in defence of the officers' breach of sanctuary. The dispute was inconclusive, but Wyclif preserved his own pleadings in a book he had just started *On the Church*. Once again, he relished the opportunity to cut down the pretensions of the hierarchy: neither God nor the Pope, he claimed, could exempt an absconding debtor from being brought to book and the clergy should not shelter such runaways. But in spite of his eloquence, the Abbey of Westminster remained a sanctuary as long as it remained an Abbey.

6   Church, King, and Pope

In 1378 and 1379 Wyclif worked on the sixth, seventh, and eighth treatises of his theological *summa*. All of them dealt with the nature of the Church, the form of its government, and its relations with the State. In the *summa* the treatises were to be read in the following order: *On the Church*, *On the Office of King*, *On the Power of the Pope*; but it is clear that they were written at about the same time, and that their chapters were not all composed in the order in which they were meant to be read. Fragments seem to have been written when Pope Gregory was still alive, others when Wyclif still trusted in the virtues of Urban VI, others when the progress of the schism was undermining Wyclif's faith not just in individual Popes but in the Papacy as an institution.

The controlling theme of the treatise *On the Church* is that the Church consists essentially of all those who are predestined to eternal bliss in heaven. There are, Wyclif tells us, three senses of the word 'Church'. It can mean a temporary gathering of those faithful who are now in a state of grace: such a gathering might be a gathering entirely of non-predestined; if so, it would not be the mystical body of Christ or any part of the holy Catholic Church. Or 'the Church' might mean a medley of predestined and non-predestined, presently in a state of grace: this coincides partly but not totally with the true Church of God. This is the Church spoken of in the gospel parables of the wise and foolish virgins and the tares growing amid the wheat. In the third sense the Church is the gathering of the predestinate, whether they are at present in a state of grace or not. This is the Church which figures in the Creed; this is the holy, glorious and unblemished Church which St Paul hymns in the Epistle to the Ephesians. Non-predestinate men and women may be *in* such a Church, but they are not *of* it.

What is this predestination which confers Church membership? Like all other theologians, Wyclif takes as his starting point the text of Romans 8:28–30.

> All things work together for good, to them that love God, to them who are the called according to his purpose. For whom he did foreknow, he also did predestinate to be conformed to the image of his son, that he might be the first born among many brethren. Moreover, whom he did predestinate them he also called; and whom he called, them he also justified; and whom he justified, them also he glorified.

The text, Wyclif says, shows us four stages of membership of the Church: vocation, predestination, justification, and glorification. Predestination is the eternal love which God has for those who are to share his bliss. Corresponding to this active predestination in God, there is a passive predestination in each predestinate person: not any entity which can exist by itself, but a relationship to God's decree.

> This predestination is the principal gift of God, most freely given, since no one can merit his own predestination. Since it cannot be present without being present at the first moment of existence of the predestinate, it follows from what is commonly said of grace that this is the principal grace . . . It can never be lost, since it is the basis of glory and bliss, which equally cannot be lost. (W 1886. 39)

Predestination, glory, and bliss are all things of which it can

be said: if ever you have them at all, you have them for ever;
in that sense they cannot be lost.

However, someone who is predestined may very well fall
into sin, as did David, Peter, and Paul, whose sins are
recorded in the Bible. Hence not everyone who is
predestinate is in a state of grace or justice all his life;
predestination does not involve continual righteousness,
but only final perseverance. Equally, someone who is non-
predestinate may be in a state of grace for the time being,
even though eventual damnation awaits him: not all those
who are now righteous are predestinate. But

> God loves Peter infinitely more even while Peter is
> denying him than he loves Iscariot while Iscariot is in
> grace. For God's love is unchangingly equal, so he
> always loves Peter to bliss, since he knows he is to be
> finally converted, and he always loves Iscariot to
> everlasting punishment, since he eternally sees all past
> and future things as present. (W 1886. 140)

Wyclif links the theory of *On the Church* with the theory
of *On Civil Dominion* that lordship depends on grace. It is
on grace, not predestination, that lordship rests. One of the
predestinate, if he sins, forfeits dominion; a non-
predestinate may enjoy it lawfully during such time as he
is in a state of grace. If ownership and office depended on
predestination, rather than lack of sin, everything would
be in a state of total confusion: we can make reasonable
conjectures as to whether prelates are sinning or not, but
only a revelation about the future could tell us whether
they were predestined or not.

> Indeed, nobody knows whether he is himself
> predestined or not. Without a special revelation no one
> should assert that he is predestined; and similarly he

should not assert that he is a member of the church, or,
for that matter its head. (W 1886. 5)

For not even the Pope knows that he is predestined, and
consequently he does not know that he is the head or even
a member of the Church in the one sense that really
matters, the Church which is the spotless bride of Christ.

In what sense *is* the Pope head of the Church? If the
Church is the body of the predestined, it is clear that it
includes many Old Testament saints and patriarchs who
lived and died long before there were any Popes. The
Church is traditionally divided into three parts:

> We speak only of the Catholic church which contains in
> itself three parts: one triumphing in heaven, one
> sleeping in purgatory, and one battling on earth. (W
> 1886. 8)

It can only be of the Church militant on earth that the Pope
can in any sense be head: and even on earth the Greek and
other Churches do not acknowledge his authority. So the
more experienced theologians affirm not that the Pope is
head of the universal Church, but only that he is head of a
particular Church – provided always that he perseveres in
living the good life that a Pope should live. The Pope is head
of as much of the Latin Church as acknowledges his rule;
and it is wrong to call 'this poor particular church cramped
in a corner' the holy Catholic Church. But if the Pope rules
it well, according to the law of Christ, as once Popes used
to do, then he and his colleagues can be called the universal
Church in embryo. But only Christ can be its head (W 1886.
94).

But did not Pope Boniface VIII in his bull *Unam Sanctam*
declare that to be subject to the Bishop of Rome was
necessary for salvation for every human creature? And did

he not claim the obedience of all secular lords to him as head of the universal Church?

No Pope short of Christ himself, says Wyclif, could have meant this in a Catholic sense; so we should not attribute to Boniface the blasphemy which he seems to have meant. Without a special revelation no Bishop of Rome should think that every Christian has to be subjected to him. For there are many Christians, of different periods, outside his jurisdiction, not to mention the foremost Christian of all. Moreover, the Pope does not know that he is predestined; and unless he is he cannot be a captain in the Church of God.

> A Christian can have grace from God without believing that there is any such Pope, because God does not have to use the Pope as his minister in the gift of grace. He can die in grace without recognizing any such subjection. In such a case salvation would have come to a Christian without subjection to the Pope. (W 1886. 32)

Popes and prelates, then, if they are not predestined, are not members of the Church; if they are not in a state of grace they forfeit their right to property and their claim to obedience. But this does not mean that they are of no service to the Church. A non-predestinate priest, even while he is in a state of sin, can validly administer the sacraments: he can baptize, ordain, hear confessions, and say Mass. In doing so he heaps up his own sin and contributes to his own damnation; but he does no harm to his charges and may indeed benefit them if they themselves are rightly disposed. But while the sacrament of penance is useful to the penitent sinner, the Papal lawyers have built up around it the absurd theory of indulgences, claiming that bishops can remit, in return for money, days and years of the punishment due to the sins God has forgiven. So

Wyclif concludes *On the Church* with an attack on the theory of indulgences; the theory which, one hundred and forty years later, was to be the first target of the Lutheran reformation.

Wyclif's theory of the Papacy is further developed in the treatise *On the Power of the Pope*. It is not a theory which is easy to summarize. Among the heresies for which Wyclif was posthumously condemned were the propositions that the Church of Rome was the synagogue of Satan, and that the Pope's excommunication was not to be feared, because it was the censure of Antichrist. And in the increasingly polemical tracts of Wyclif's last years, and in many of his sermons, there are endlessly repeated attacks on the Popes and on the exaggerated claims made for Papal power. But Wyclif's most carefully thought-out treatment of the topic, in his *summa*, is far from taking a wholly negative view of the Papacy as a Christian institution, however much individual Popes may be identified as Antichrists.

In these treatises Wyclif denounces in strong terms the sins of Gregory XI.

A man may be reputed the Vicar of Christ by all human solemnity, rite, and reputation, and yet be a fearful devil, as it is not beyond belief in the case of Gregory XI and his like. For if a man used the tithes and goods of the English poor to marry off his nephew to an heiress, and supported the families of many of his kinsfolk in worldly pomp, and bought his brother out of just imprisonment, and had many thousand men killed for worldly gain, and did not finally repent, who can doubt that he was a perpetual heretic and never a head or member of mother church? . . . I do not sit in judgement upon him, as some ecclasiastical superiors do; but I say that neither he nor anyone else is Vicar of Christ or of Peter unless he leaves worldly ways and imitates their conduct; and thus it is possible for a pretended Bishop of Rome to be the head of the members of the devil. (W 1886. 366)

This is strong language: but it can be paralleled by that of canonized saints. St Catherine of Siena told Gregory to his face that his court of Avignon stank like hell, and St Bridget of Sweden had a vision in which the Lord spoke to the Pope saying, 'Thou dost rob me of innumerable souls; for almost all who come to thy court dost thou cast into the hell of fire.' And Wyclif's own denunciation of Gregory is followed by his calling a blessing on the spouse of the Church who has killed Gregory, scattered his accomplices, and revealed his crimes to the Church through Urban VI.

When Wyclif calls particular Popes Antichrists, he does not mean that the Papacy as such is an antichristian institution: rather, just as the office of Pope calls for unparalleled holiness in its possessors, so it gives them unparalleled power of doing harm to the Church. *On the Power of the Pope*, after a philosophical disquisition on the nature of power, examines the position of St Peter in respect of the other Apostles and the early Church. Wyclif agrees that Peter enjoyed a certain primacy, and passed on this primacy to his successors, so that there continues to be a captain in the Church militant. But what is the relation between the succession to St Peter and the Bishopric of Rome?

We certainly cannot say that the succession to Peter is automatically conferred by human election. indeed election is a poor way of choosing any bishop and it might be better to draw lots between the candidates. What does the word 'Pope' mean? It is not a biblical term, and it was once used of bishops other than the Bishop of Rome. It has come to mean the bishop who bears the most high and most

Christlike role; and this is commonly said to be the Roman bishop. But the Papacy, so understood, is not necessarily the same thing as the Roman episcopate. Rome may be the capital of Christendom, but the Pope need not live there; Peter did not always do so, nor did the Popes who grew fat in Avignon. The emperor could not attach the Papacy eternally to Rome, any more than the Emperor of Tartary, if he was converted to Christianity, could make the church of Cambalek in Cathay the head of all the other churches.

It is necessary that there should always be a Pope in the Church militant; but a man can only be Pope if he keeps within the limits set by St Peter, whether he be Bishop of Rome or elsewhere. He should be poor, and free from worldly concerns: he should be able to say, like Peter, 'Silver and gold have I none'. The Pope should not interfere in worldly matters; he should feed the flock of Christ by preaching, prayer, and the example of holiness. The Pope should be believed more than others; but that should be because of his sanctity of life and his following Christ more closely than others. If a Roman bishop wanders from this path, why should his word be trusted more than that of the ancient saints who were not bishops of Rome? The Pope can be rebuked by others; to deny this is to say that he is either an impeccable Christ or an incorrigible Lucifer. Indeed since a Pope is more subject to temptation than others, more care should be taken to see that he is open to correction and reproof.

It is difficult to recognize in the rival Popes of today the lineaments of the ideal successor of St Peter. It is easier to see in the present times a fulfilment of Christ's prediction of the last days: 'Then if any man shall say unto you, Lo here is Christ or there, believe it not. For there shall arise false Christs and false prophets, and shall shew great signs and wonders' (Mt. 24:23–4).

It seems to me that this prophecy can be expounded as fitting those who today say they are Popes: for each of them says he is Christ and God, and of greater or ampler power than our Jesus; in whose name they claim to speak as his supreme vicars . . .

We should not believe the mere words of those who say now that the Pope is at Rome, now that he is at Avignon, but we should believe works which conform to Christ. (W 1907. 149)

Until it is revealed to the Church which is the true Pope, the children of God should wait in peace, ready in due course to give due obedience. We should not swear to either of them for fear we are swearing to Antichrist.

The Catholic truth which I have often repeated consists in this: that no pope, bishop, abbot, or any spiritual prelate is to be believed or obeyed except in so far as he says or commands the law of Christ; consequently neither Urban nor Robert is someone whom the faithful are bound to believe, except in so far as they tell the faith of scripture; nor is it part of the substance of faith to believe explicitly that either of them is Pope. Blessed be the God of truth, who ordained this schism so that the truth of this faith might shine out. (W 1907. 149)

It may be that not just one, but both of them are Antichrists; the supporters of the Avignon claimant can offer no convincing evidence that he is Pope, nor can we prove from his works or from revelation that our Roman bishop is the Pope. So it seems safe to say that it would be better for the Church to have none such, and that we should live as before the endowment of the Church, when its government was in common (W 1907. 186).

It was indeed the endowment of the Roman Church that

was the beginning of corruption. Wyclif, like his contemporaries, believed that the temporal power of the Pope derived from a gift by the Emperor Constantine to the Pope who baptized him, Saint Silvester. The story of the donation of Constantine would, within a few decades of Wyclif's writing, be exposed as a forgery by an official at the Vatican; but Wyclif does not question its truth. The gift of Constantine, he maintained, was an infusion of poison into the Church. Endowment led Popes into heresy, and led to the multiplication of clerical degrees and clerical discord. Before this, on the evidence of Jerome, there was no difference between bishops and priests, as was the case in the early Church, as we know from the writings of Paul.

Wyclif's description of the evils consequent on Papal endowment is merely an application of his general thesis that the clergy should not be endowed at all: a thesis first stated in *On Civil Dominion*, repeated in *On the Church*, and reinforced in the *On the Office of King*. In the latter work the duty of reform in this matter is assigned to the secular ruler. As is the case with many of Wyclif's later works, the content of this disquisition on Church and State appears not only in the Latin treatise from his pen, but also in English abbreviations which have often been attributed to him, and published as his English works. Scholars nowadays are more inclined to regard these English texts as the work of his disciples. But I shall quote from an English Wycliffite treatise on the function of the secular ruler, both to give an indication of the contents of *On the Office of King*, and to give the flavour of the English of Wyclif's circle.

It is said in Latin what office Popes should have, and what should be the office of kings by the law of God; and for to make this thing more known, is somewhat told in English. Three things move men to speak of king's office: first, for kings may hereby see that they should not be idle but rule by God's law to win the bliss of heaven; the second is that kings should not be tyrants of their people, but rule them by reason that falls to their state; the third cause is most of all, for thus should God's law be better known, for therein is man's help both of body and soul that evermore shall last.

The writer illustrates from the Gospel that Christians should be subject to kings and secular lords.

Christ chose to be born when the emperor flourished most; Christ chose to be worshipped and sustained by three kings; Christ paid tallage to the emperor; Christ taught to pay to the emperor what was his; Christ chose to be buried solemnly of knights, and he committed his church to the government of knights. And therefore teaches Peter that Christian men should be subject in all meekness to all manner of men, as to kings as passing before other men, and to dukes as next under kings; and these be in status to perform these offices; to take vengeance on evil men and to praise good men.

Kings are then compared with Popes, to the disadvantage, naturally, of the latter.

Many such words speaks God's law of kings, but it speaks not of Popes, neither good nor evil. But when venom of endowment was entered into the church was the name of Pope founded; that sounded wonderful, for it were a great wonder that Christ should make his vicar the man that most contraries him in manner of living. Well I wot that the Pope is nothing sib to Peter but if he live a poor life and a meek as Peter did, and pass in feeding of Christ's sheep, with teaching of the gospel. (H 129)

7   The body of Christ

It was not Wyclif's assault on the Papacy which led to his final breach with the teaching authority of the Church. It was when he turned to the sacrament of the Eucharist, and attacked the theologians' explanation of its nature, that he began to stand out in clear view as a heretic. When he denounced the Popes and questioned the validity of Papal claims he could find sympathizers even among the higher clergy; when he called for the disendowment of the Church, many laymen and begging friars found his words congenial; but when he renounced the doctrine of transubstantiation, friars, noblemen, and bishops all turned against him, and the university which had hitherto sheltered him offered him a home no longer. Events were to take a similar course nationally in the Reformation of the sixteenth century. Bishops who went along cheerfully with Henry VIII when he threw off allegiance to the Pope and despoiled abbeys and priories were prepared, in the days of his son, to go to prison rather than accept any meddling with the Mass.

For most of his life, Wyclif accepted the traditional doctrine of the Eucharist. He never ceased to venerate as a great sacrament the rite instituted by Jesus when at his last supper he took bread and said 'This is my body' and took wine and said 'This is my blood'. When, probably in 1379, Wyclif began to give the lectures which caused such a sensation, it was not the doctrine of the Real Presence that he was attacking, but the doctrine of transubstantiation as currently explained. The two doctrines are often confused by those unfamiliar with Catholic theology, but they must be kept carefully distinct by anyone who wishes to understand Wyclif.

We may ask about the Eucharist two questions. First, do the words 'This is my body', uttered by Christ or his priest, make the body of Christ really and not just symbolically present? If you answer yes to that question, then you believe in the doctrine of the Real Presence. We may then go on to ask: What happens to the bread? Is it still there? To accept the doctrine of transubstantiation you have to give a negative answer: it is no longer there; it has been turned into the body of Christ. Believers in transubstantiation may then go on to give a number of different answers to the further question why the host continues to look and taste like bread, and what it is that the communicant sees and tastes.

The Catholic doctrine against which Wyclif was rebelling was codified, two centuries later, by the counter-reformation Council of Trent. Its essential elements are summed up in the Catechism of that Council.

Now there are three wonderful and stupendous things which in this Sacrament, Holy Church without all doubt believes and confesses to be wrought by the words of consecration. The First is, That the true Body of Christ, that very same which was born of the Virgin, and now sits in Heaven at the Right-hand of the Father is contain'd in this Sacrament. The Second is that no substance of the Elements remains in it: altho' nothing seems more strange and distant to the senses. The Third, which is easily gather'd from both the former, tho the words of Consecration fully express it, is that what is beheld by the Eyes, or perceiv'd by the other Senses is in a wonderful and unspeakable manner, without any subject matter. And one may see indeed all the

Accidents of Bread and Wine, which yet are inherent in no substance, but they consist of themselves; because the Substance of Bread and Wine is so chang'd into the Body and Blood of the Lord, that the substance of the Bread and Wine altogether ceases.

Unlike some of the sixteenth-century reformers, Wyclif throughout his life accepted the first of these three 'wonderful and stupendous things'; it was against the second and third that the attacks of his last years were directed.

Between 1380 and his death Wyclif published no less than six tracts which refer to the Eucharist in their titles; and the tenth of the treatises in his theological *summa*, *On Apostasy*, is largely devoted despite its title to a discussion of Eucharistic errors. But the fullest account of his theories is to be found in the treatise *On the Eucharist*, which is the published version of the momentous lecture course which led to his expulsion from Oxford. It is one of Wyclif's most vigorous writings, exhibiting at the same time his philosophical acumen, his familiarity with the Bible and the Fathers, and his sweeping historical approach to questions of Church doctrine. The tone of the criticism of his adversaries is comparatively restrained, and there are comparatively few digressions on hobby horses such as clerical disendowment.

Wyclif's objections to current teaching on the Eucharist are both philosophical and theological. Philosophically, the theory that accidents can exist without a substance leads to many absurdities; theologically, the doctrine of transubstantiation is a novelty imposed on the faithful in recent centuries. It is not only a superfluous addition to the creeds, but contradicts the teaching of the Fathers, especially of St Augustine.

For many years Wyclif had been concerned about the relationship between Eucharistic doctrine and his denial of the possibility of annihilation. When he wrote his philosophical treatise on the creative power of God, he denied that transubstantiation involved annihilation: the substance of bread and wine did not vanish into nothing, since the accidents remained. Now, having ceased to believe in transubstantiation, he uses the impossibility of annihilation as one of many arguments against his opponents. But though Scotus and Ockham and most recent scholastics believed that in the Eucharist the substance of bread and wine was annihilated, St Thomas Aquinas, as Wyclif knew, had denied that any annihilation took place. A loyal Catholic was not bound to believe in annihilation, provided that he could explain the miraculous conversion of bread and wine in some other way.

But it was common to all the standard accounts of the Eucharist that the accidents remained without a substance. The colour and shape of the sacramental host were not accidents inhering in the bread, for the bread was no longer there; nor were they accidents of the body of Christ, otherwise that would be white and round like the host. It is this theory of accidents without a substance which Wyclif regarded as quintessentially absurd, and he devised argument after argument to bring out the absurdity.

> To talk of accidents without a substance is self-contradictory. Every accident which formally inheres in a substance is nothing other than the truth that the substance is such-and-such in an accidental manner; but there cannot be such a truth without a substance, any more than there can be a creature without God; so there

is no such thing as a heap of accidents without a subject which is the consecrated host. (W 1892. 63)

Any whiteness must be the whiteness of something; but the whiteness of X is simply the truth that X is white; just as you cannot have a truth which is just the predicate '. . . is white' without a subject, so you cannot have an accident without a substance.

If qualities could exist separately, Wyclif says, then we should venerate the virtues of the saints rather than the saints themselves; for it is only because of their virtues, after all, that we honour the saints. Faith, hope, charity, and felicity would be holy maidens we could pray to: they would have, of their nature, the qualities that the saints only have by acquisition. Moreover, if qualities can exist all on their own, then *a fortiori* they could exist in a non-standard subject; God in his omnipotence might endow a log or a pebble with a most subtle intellect and the most supreme happiness.

> But these are mere ravings, because a quality is nothing other than a subject's being qualified, and a form is nothing other than a substance's being enformed; thus it is the same thing to maintain that a quality is all by itself without a substance as it is to say that a substance is such-and-such without being a substance; and thus the notion that there is an accident without a substance for its subject includes a formal contradiction. (W 1892. 201)

All scholastics agreed that in the Eucharist there were accidents without a substance; but opinions differed as to which was the primary self-subsistent accident which constituted or underlay the host. There are three opinions, Wyclif says, in the churches of Britain. In the province of

Canterbury they say that the host is weight; in the Lincoln diocese they say that it is quantity; in Wales and Ireland they say that it is whiteness – but then in Ireland, says Wyclif, with a rare attempt at humour, they see dead men walk. The Lincoln theory seems to be that of St Thomas who says that in the host there remains the extension of the bread, which is the subject of form, colour, taste, and other observable phenomena. This seems to have been Wyclif's own view as long as he believed in transubstantiation, for he then regarded the host as 'a mathematical body'.

If you believe in the possibility of accidents without substance, Wyclif now argues, you have no reason to believe in the existence of material substances at all.

> On this theory no intellect or sense proves the existence of any material substance; because no matter what sense-experience or cognition is present, it is possible and consistent that the whole created universe is just a ball of accidents; so someone who wishes to posit material objects must rely on the faith of Scripture. (W 1892. 78)

Believers in transubstantiation, then, are reduced to a position of phenomenalism: except where scripture tells us the contrary, the world may be nothing but appearance. But scripture does not tell us even of our own existence. No doubt each of us is self-conscious, but self-consciousness does not tell me that I have a body as well as a soul; neither sense nor reason, if Wyclif's opponents are right, can show me that I exist.

> So of each of us it should be piously doubted whether he exists, and what he is. This would make it very difficult to examine the work of the clergy, to count the number of monks, and to list the coins and gifts they have been

given. Because each person could be a spirit linked to
bare accidents, in which case he would not be the kind
of man we know. (W 1892. 79)

But this whole theory turns God into a deceiver. The
theologians postulate the continuance of the accidents, so
as to avoid having to say that the senses are deceived; but
if there is no bread and wine there, then there is an even
more grievous deception of our inner judgement.

> Since the senses of men, both inner and outer, judge that
> what remains is bread and wine exactly like
> unconsecrated stuff, it seems that it is unworthy of the
> lord of truth to introduce such an illusion in his gracious
> giving of so worthy a gift. (W 1892. 57)

A philosopher who reads these passages of Wyclif cannot
help but be reminded of Descartes. Descartes, like the
opponent Wyclif sets up, thinks that all the deliverances
of inner and outer senses are, in themselves, compatible
with the non-existence of the external world. Only the
veracity of God, he maintains, convinces us of the reality
of body as well as mind. And human beings, as conceived
by Descartes, are indeed spirits linked to bare accidents; for
the only matter which he recognizes is bare extension, the
mathematical body of the youthful Wyclif. Cartesian man,
it seems, is Wyclif's invention.

Wyclif's anti-Cartesian points are well taken; but he goes
further in trying to convict his adversaries of absurdity.
Those who say that they see Christ in the sacrament should
tell us whether he is standing or sitting, and tell us what
colour and size he is in the different hosts. Is he lighter in
one and darker in another, big in one and small in another?
Must not Christ move in six different ways at once if four
priests carry the host to four points of the compass, and one

lifts it up and another puts it down? These questions may seem unfair taunts, because it was not part of the theory of Wyclif's opponents that the accidents of the host inhered in the substance of Christ; it was precisely to avoid saying that the whiteness of the host was the whiteness of Christ that the theory of self-subsistent accidents was introduced. But, Wyclif says, if the link between Christ's body and the accidents of the host is broken, then how does the presence of the host on the altar effect the presence of Christ on the altar? For being in a place is an accident just as much as being white or being round or being an inch in diameter.

Wyclif's philosophical arguments against transubstantiation are powerful. But his opposition to the doctrine is based also on theological grounds: it is an unscriptural innovation. St Thomas Aquinas may have taught it, though – says Wyclif – it is more charitable to suppose that his works were tampered with after his death by evil friars. But if he did teach it, it was a rash doctrine to teach, and quite unproved.

> It is rash, because it sets out as an article of faith that neither bread nor wine remain after the consecration; which is excessively rash for many reasons; for it is an article which occurs in none of the three creeds of the church. What plausibility is there in saying that because of the rash assertion of one man the church is to be burdened with a new article of faith? (W 1892. 140)

In Wyclif's time the doctrine of transubstantiation had not, of course, been defined by the Council of Trent; and it was only in response to his own teaching that the Council of Constance after his death asserted that in the sacrament there were accidents without substance. There were two main official documents which set the limits of orthodox debate in the fourteenth century: the recantations imposed upon the Eucharistic heretic Berengar in the eleventh century, and the reference in the fourth Lateran Council of 1215 to 'the sacrifice of Jesus Christ, whose body and blood in the sacrament of the altar truly is contained under the appearances of bread and wine, the bread being transubstantiated into the body, and the wine into blood, by the divine power'.

Wyclif showed that no compelling proof of transubstantiation could be found in scripture, and that the Church Fathers, and especially Augustine, were perfectly happy to speak of the sacrament after consecration as bread; as, indeed, was St Paul. The ecclesiastical authorities had found Berengar a difficult man to pin down: he had been made to swear at different times to various different formulae, and Wyclif often cited a version subscribed to under Pope Nicholas II: 'I confess that the bread and wine which are placed on the altar after the consecration are not only the sacrament, but also the true body and blood of our Lord.' This, said Wyclif, was perfectly in accord with his own doctrine. If the Lateran Council spoke otherwise, well, its authority was less since it came later, in any case it was presided over by that thoroughly undesirable character, Pope Innocent III. The Church of Rome may have erred in this case as it has done in other cases. But, in any event, transubstantiation can be given a harmless sense, if we choose to do so, in which it does not involve accidents remaining without a substance.

Wyclif's own view is that the bread remains after the consecration; the visible and tangible accidents, after as before, are accidents of the bread. None the less, it does truly become the body of Christ, and Wyclif uses a number of illustrations to show how this can come about.

When writers write letters, words and sentences, the

paper and ink remain beneath the symbols. But through custom and skill those who can read pay much more attention to the significance of the symbols than to the natural characteristics of the signs to which an illiterate person would attend. Much more so the habit of faith brings the faithful to grasp through the consecrated bread the true body of Christ. (W 1892. 144)

The bread is not numerically identical with the body of Christ; but it is not a mere symbol either. Christ did indeed speak figuratively at the last supper, but with an efficacy not to be found on other occasions of figurative speech: 'for it has the efficacy of making the body of Christ and his blood exist in fact beneath the sacramental appearances' (W 1892. 84). When we see the host we should not believe that it is itself the body of Christ, but that the body of Christ is sacramentally hidden in it. The priest does not make the body of Christ; he makes the host be its sign or covering.

Christ is in the host as in a sign, otherwise the host would not be a sacrament; but he is not in the signs in a way which means he is not really and truly there according to his whole humanity; and so it is granted that Christ is there not only as in a sign, but more efficaciously than in a sign; nor is it inconsistent, but perfectly consistent, that one and the same thing should be both a truth and a figure or sign. (W 1892. 115)

From this time onwards, the doctrine of the Eucharist became for Wyclif the touchstone to judge all other matters. He would follow either of the rival Popes if they could tell him the truth about the nature of the Sacrament; on the other hand, if monks and friars who supported him on other matters differed from him on this, that proved that they were limbs of Satan. And if it was on this point that he judged others, it was to be on this that he was himself to be judged and condemned, after all his previous escapes. Among the many English writings which are, with greater or less plausibility, attributed to Wyclif one which has a greater claim to authenticity than most is his profession of Eucharistic belief. We may end the chapter with this summary of his faith.

I acknowledge that the sacrament of the altar is very God's body in form of bread, but it is in another manner God's body than it is in heaven. For in heaven it is seven foot in form and figure of flesh and blood. But in the sacrament God's body is by miracle of God in form of bread, and is he neither of seven foot, nor in man's figure. But as a man leaves for to think the kind of an image, whether it be of oak or of ash, and sets his thought in him of whom is the image, so much more should a man leave to think on the kind of bread. But think upon Christ, for his body is the same bread that is the sacrament of the altar, and with all cleanness, all devotion and all charity that God would give him, worship he Christ, and then he receives God ghostly more worthily than the priest that sings the mass in less charity. For the bodily eating not profits nought to soul but in as much as the soul is fed with charity. This sentence is proved by Christ that may not lie. For as the gospel says, Christ that night that he was betrayed of Judas Iscariot, he took bread in his hands, and blessed it, break it, and gave it to his disciples to eat; for he says, and may not lie, 'This is my body'. (H 17)

8 The end of the heretic

Wyclif's lectures on the Eucharist quickly lost him friends. The friars in particular, natural allies against prelates' excessive wealth, who had had their own troubles with the Popes, were deeply scandalized. One in Cambridge who had copied out with enthusiasm an anti-papal passage from *On the Power of the Pope*, noting 'these are the words of the venerable doctor, Master John Wyclif', within the year altered 'venerable doctor' to 'accursed seducer'. In Oxford the friars organized lectures and debates in the defence of the Eucharistic teaching of the Franciscans Scotus and Ockham. In the spring of 1380 William Barton, the Chancellor of the University, set up a commission of twelve doctors to examine Wyclif's doctrine. By a majority the commissioners condemned two propositions: that the substance of bread and wine remain after the consecration, and that the body of Christ is not corporally but figuratively present in the sacrament. These theses were said to be dangerous to the Catholic faith and damaging to the reputation of the University: anyone teaching them was threatened with imprisonment, suspension from University functions, and excommunication. The sentence was brought to Wyclif as he was lecturing in the class-room of the Austin friars; he was distressed by the news, but said 'that neither the chancellor nor any of his accomplices could weaken his opinion'.

Wyclif made some attempt to appeal to the King against the sentence. John of Gaunt travelled to Oxford in person to urge him to hold his peace on the topic. But Wyclif set about writing a reaffirmation and defence of his position, the *Confession*, which he published in May 1381. Henceforth he could no longer count on support at Court.

Worse was to follow. In the same month there broke out in protest against an unpopular poll-tax an insurrection, which is commonly known as the Peasants' Revolt. Wat Tyler led the Kentish rebels in a march on London, and Archbishop Sudbury of Canterbury was murdered. During the ferocious suppression of the rebellion one of the leaders, John Ball (known to every schoolchild for his subversive couplet 'When Adam delved and Eve span / Who was then the gentleman?') was reported to have confessed, before execution, 'that for two years he had been a disciple of Wyclif, and had learned from him the heresies he had taught'. The story is no doubt false, but the revolutionaries would not have been doing violence to the text of *On Civil Dominion* if they had claimed its support for the expropriation of the wicked rich. The doctrine that sin forfeited dominion could well have been applied to the property and offices of the lay nobility, whose misdeeds were no less flagrant than those of the clergy. But Wyclif had been cautiously, indeed embarrassingly, reluctant to draw the parallel, and he could hardly have had any practical involvement in the revolt. However, he did have the courage to plead in favour of the peasants after the revolt had been put down. He was prepared to justify up to a point the killing of the Archbishop: his death was a just, though cruel, punishment for his worldliness. Ironically, the murder of the Archbishop did him an ill turn, for Sudbury was succeeded by Courtenay, Wyclif's old opponent, who, as Bishop of London, had tried to silence him four years earlier.

Shortly after the peasants' revolt, Wyclif decided to leave Oxford. He resided until his death in the rectory at

Lutterworth, to which he was presented in 1374. One of his last acts at Oxford was to pawn his copy of the Papal decretals, the manual of Canon Law. The volumes of the Church Fathers he took with him to Lutterworth.

During his last days in Oxford and his earliest days in Lutterworth Wyclif completed the final portion of his theological *summa*. It was a self-contained trilogy on three kinds of heresy: *On Simony*, *On Apostasy*, and *On Blasphemy*. Simony was the sin of purchasing ecclesiastical office; it was, no doubt, a prevalent vice, but in Wyclif's hands 'Simony' acquires such a broad sense as to mean any kind of clerical worldliness, negligence, or unworthiness. The forms of apostasy which he singles out for attack are the failure of the religious orders to live up to their vocation, and the Eucharistic teaching of the supporters of transubstantiation. *On Blasphemy* is a bilious and repetitive catalogue of the delinquencies of churchmen at every level of the ecclesiastical hierarchy. Taking as his text the verse of Proverbs, 'The horseleech has two daughters, crying "give, give" ' (Prov. 39:15), Wyclif tells us that the devil is a bloodsucking leech with twelve greedy daughters: the Pope, his cardinals, the bishops, the archdeacons, the chancellors, the deans, the rectors, the priests, the monks, the friars, the clerks, and the tithe-collectors. The clergy of each of these ranks are tormentors of the Church; we are taken through, chapter by chapter, the scourges inflicted by each group. Thus we learn of greedy archdeacons exceeding their canonical allowance of seven horses, and of rural deans encouraging prostitutes so that they can make a fat income by fining their clients. The groups most bitterly attacked are the cardinals and the friars. 'Cardinal', we are told, is an acronym for Captain of the Apostates of the Realm of the Devil, Impudent and Nefarious Ally of Lucifer. Friars are greedy, idle, blasphemous seducers, whose sins are aggravated by their hypocritical pretensions to virtue. For them too, there is an appropriate acronym: Carmelites, Augustinians, Jacobites (i.e. Dominicans), and Minorites (i.e. Franciscans) spell, with their initial letters, the name of the first murderer CAIM: their convents are Caim's castles.

From this time until his death Wyclif waged war on the friars, pouring out a flood of abuse against them in pamphlets and sermons. He never forgave them for driving him out of Oxford. When he left for Lutterworth, he left behind a number of friends who were willing to continue to fight in the University in his defence. Two of the most eloquent were Nicholas of Hereford, the translator of the Bible, and Philip Repton, a canon from Leicester about to take his doctorate. Moreover, after Wyclif's departure the Chancellor who had condemned him was succeeded by a new and more sympathetic Chancellor, Robert Rigg. In February 1382 Hereford preached in St Mary's, to the effect that members of religious orders should not take degrees in the University. Chancellor Rigg, so far from disciplining him, appointed him to preach the University sermon on Ascension Day. Hereford used the occasion to defend Wyclif's teaching.

Meanwhile, Archbishop Courtenay was losing no time in proceeding against the new heresies. Ten days after his appointment was confirmed by the Pope, he summoned a gathering of bishops and theologians to Blackfriars in London and laid before them twenty-four propositions drawn from Wyclif's writings. Four days later, on 21 May, the council condemned ten of these as heretical and censured fourteen less severely as 'erroneous'. The heresies concerned the Eucharist, the limits of the sacramental powers of the clergy, the dispensability of the Papacy, and

the wickedness of clerical endowment. The proceedings
were interrupted by an earthquake. Wyclif, when he heard
of this, naturally interpreted it as a sign of God's displeasure
at an unjust verdict. Archbishop Courtenay, however, rose
to the occasion and explained to his colleagues that it was
merely a symbol that the realm was breaking wind of the
foul heresies that had been bottled up in it.

Wyclif was not condemned by name, and neither then
nor later was he excommunicated. But his followers were
to be disciplined. Courtenay had a decree tacked on to an
Act of Parliament calling for the arrest and imprisonment
of unlicensed itinerant preachers; and he sent a Carmelite
friar to Oxford to promulgate the Blackfriars decision on
Corpus Christi day (5 June). The friar handed his
commission to the Chancellor, but found him unwilling
to publish it; instead he had to listen to a sermon by Philip
Repton maintaining that Wyclif's doctrine of the
sacrament of the altar was that of the whole Church of God.
It would be more than his life was worth, the friar told the
archbishop, to publish the condemnation; the University
was literally up in arms in defence of its privileges.

But the University's show of independence was short-
lived. Chancellor Rigg, whose loyalty to Wyclif was always
in direct proportion to his distance from the Archbishop of
Canterbury, was quickly brought to his knees when
summoned before the Privy Council. He endorsed the
condemnation of the twenty-four theses, and accepted
orders forbidding Wyclif, Hereford, Repton, and their
friends from lecturing or preaching until they had purged
themselves of heresy. Returning to Oxford, he published
the Blackfriars decrees in St Mary's; he plucked up courage
to add a censure on an anti-Wycliffite doctor who had called
Hereford and his friends 'Lollards'. The word was a
contemptuous one, meaning 'mumbler'; in spite of Rigg's

censure, it became the name by which supporters of Wyclif's heresies were henceforth to be known.

Before the year was over, support for Wyclif in Oxford had been stamped out. Hereford and Repton were excommunicated at St Paul's in July: Hereford fled abroad to appeal to the Pope; Repton, in November, recanted his errors before the convocation of Canterbury assembled in Oxford. His recantation was the prelude to a glittering ecclesiastical career: he ended his days as Bishop of Lincoln, and a zealous uprooter of Lollardry. Rumours were put about that Wyclif had himself recanted; but there is no clinching evidence for this, and the recantations placed in his mouth by chroniclers are in fact resolute statements of the doctrines for which he had been condemned. We do, however, have his own word for it that he made a promise to avoid using his more offensive Eucharistic terminology outside an academic context. Perhaps this was why he was allowed to end his days in peace at Lutterworth. Whatever the reason, Courtenay, victorious, was not vindictive.

Until his death Wyclif continued to expound his doctrines both in slender pamphlets and in bulky tracts. He devoted much time to the editing and publishing of his sermons. Some were sermons already delivered in Oxford, and others can be dated to particular occasions in his final years. But most of Wyclif's sermons – cycles for the Sunday gospels and epistles, homilies for saints' days and great feasts – seem rather to have been model sermons for the general use of preachers. Many of them are extant both in Latin and in a modified English version. How far the vernacular versions are his own work and how far the work of his admirers is a question that still awaits scholarly decision. The sermons are for the most part straightforward homilies on the biblical texts; free, for better or worse, from the anecdotes and topical allusions that enlivened most medieval sermons. But all too often Wyclif uses an episode in Christ's life, or a scriptural text, merely as a peg on which to hang an attack on his *bêtes noires*. He is to preach on Good Friday. Does he treat of the sufferings of the Saviour, or of the redemptive value of his death? No: he takes as his text Judas' words 'Hail, Master' so that he can denounce the mendicants and the rival Popes. On Easter Sunday, again, he chooses to preach on the nature of the Eucharist: honest burghers, he says, do not let friars enter their wine cellars for fear they bless the wine and turn every barrel into mere accidents. Even a Christmas sermon begins with an attack on mercenary Papal canonization.

In general, Wyclif's last writings add little to the content of his major Oxford works. But he experimented with new literary forms. A rather stilted *Dialogue* between Truth and Falsehood preceded a much more successful *Trialogue* in which he presented a summary of his theological *summa*. Wyclif clearly thought that 'dialogue' meant a conversation between two people; so in the Trialogue there are three characters, Alithia, Pseustis, and Phronesis, representing truth, falsehood, and wisdom. Here, in reaction to the Blackfriars condemnation he restates his characteristic theological positions. There are four books: one on the nature of God, one on the world, one on virtues, vices, and salvation; and one on the nature of signs and sacraments. The proportions of the work are less distorted by controversy than is usual in Wyclif's later writings. This, his last completed major book, became one of the most popular of his works: it was printed in 1525, 1753, and 1869 while almost all his other writings survived only in manuscript.

The one interesting new development in Wyclif's last years was his espousal of pacifism. In *On the Office of the King* he had set out the conditions for a just war; and he had been a supporter, though not an uncritical one, of taxes raised for the war against France. But now something happened to change his attitude to war-making. In 1383 the Bishop of Norwich was commissioned by Pope Urban to lead a crusade against the adherents of the French antipope in Flanders. The crusade, in spite of the indulgences offered to reward support, was an ignominious failure. To Wyclif it was paradigm of all that was worldly and wicked in the Papacy of the schism. He denounced it in a series of pamphlets and sermons; and from the denunciation of the particular evils of this crusade, he went on, in one of his last sermons, to the proscription of all war.

To choose war is to choose the way of the devil rather than of Christ, and is to display lack of faith. War can always be avoided by those who are willing to give up worldly honours and worldly wealth. Warfare violates charity in sixteen different ways.

> It is clear that someone who engages in war of the usual kind strips himself of the rule of charity. Since someone bare of charity is excluded from the kingdom, it is clear that whoever thus wages war, in exchange for the empty or slight good of war gives away for nothing the bliss he might have more freely and easily. (W 1890. 35)

At the time of his death, Wyclif was working on a book known by the Latin title of *'Opus Evangelicum'*. Its first volume is a commentary on the Sermon on the Mount, built largely out of quotations from Augustine, Chrysostom, and Grosseteste. The second volume purports to be a commentary on Matthew: 23-5; but it has the subtitle 'On Antichrist' and is largely a repetition of familiar polemical themes.

During his last days at Lutterworth, Wyclif turned his thoughts again to Oxford. In a letter to his students there, he recalls the fresh meadows and pleasant streams, the soft airs that make the city a dwelling fit for angels, a house of God and gate of heaven. But this nostalgic memory does not distract from his polemical intent: the University had been corrupted by the friars, and its colleges should therefore be abolished. As a historian of the friars has written:

> Even this sweet Oxford had been deflowered by the friars; they had cast its prophet forth; he was an exile who would never see its spires again. Rue, not snapdragon, clung to the walls of Balliol, and the rector of Lutterworth swept his earliest home, along with Caim's castles, out from the new Jerusalem.

Wyclif's prolific output in these last years is astonishing, for soon after he retired to Lutterworth he was partially paralysed by a stroke. Some have seen here the explanation of the querulous tone of his later works. Two years later the stroke was followed by another, fatal one. He was hearing Mass on Holy Innocents Day in 1384, when, as his curate tells us,

> at the time of the elevation of the host he fell down smitten by a severe paralysis, especially in the tongue so that neither then nor afterwards could he speak.

Three days later, on the last day of 1384, he died. Since he was not under the ban of the Church, he was buried peacefully in Lutterworth churchyard; his bones rested there until they were dug up and burnt in 1428 after his posthumous condemnation. His enemies noted that he had died on the feast of St Silvester, 'against whom he had venomously barked for dotation of the Church'.

9 The afterlife of the reformer

The life of John Wyclif falls into a pattern which was to be repeated, not once but twice, in the lives of great Oxford men of other centuries. A fine product of the schools stands out among his contemporaries for learning and austerity of life. He makes a name for himself as a preacher in St Mary's. He forms around himself a group of disciples, and seems likely to dominate, by his personal influence and reputation, the course of the University's thought and practice. He then takes a doctrinal step which alienates his closest theological allies and vindicates the suspicions of his critics. Henceforth, he fights by other methods, and with other companions, the battle against irreligion: he finds himself in conflict with the men who had been his closest comrades-in-arms. Exiled from Oxford, he carries on his religious mission elsewhere, tireless in preaching, writing, and controversy, casting only a rare nostalgic glance at the distant spires of the home of his youth and promise. Such was the life of Wyclif: such too, in every detail, were the lives of John Wesley and John Henry Newman.

Mgr. Ronald Knox, who in his book *Enthusiasm* pointed out the close parallels between Wesley and Newman, applies to each of them a description which would apply equally well to Wyclif: 'a man so far in reaction from the tendencies of his age that he seems a living commentary on them, yet so much the child of his age that you cannot think of him as fitting in with any other'. Wyclif stands out from other reformers by his loyalty to scholasticism; he stands out from other scholastics by the freedom with which he criticizes the Church. He stood in a unique position in the history of thought, at the break-up of the international scholastic community and the beginning of the separate vernacular cultures. In this way he was totally a man of one age: yet, like Wesley and Newman, he continued to speak to generations yet unborn.

Like the other two Oxford Churchmen, Wyclif was to have his lasting influence outside Oxford and among non-academics. The main thrust of Oxford Lollardy had already been checked by Wyclif's death, though it revived in later decades. Early in the following century a few heads of houses were Lollards, and in 1406 someone well versed in the University's customs forged a decree of congregation praising Wyclif as 'a stout and valiant champion of the faith' and affirming that 'amongst all the rest of the university he had written in logic, philosophy, divinity, morality, and the speculative arts, without his peer'. In 1409 the Archbishop of Canterbury appointed a commission to identify errors in Wyclif's works and to free the University from the remains of Lollard infection; from 1412 onwards all masters had to swear not to teach his characteristic doctrines.

Outside the University in the reign of Richard II there was an influential group of knights who were reputed Lollards; their numbers seem to have been reduced after the passing in 1401 of the statute *De Heretico Comburendo*, which decreed that obdurate supporters of heresies such as Wyclif's should be tried by the Church, handed over to the secular authorities, and burnt. The most persevering of Wyclif's disciples were working-class folk led by simple priests, who gathered in conventicles in town and countryside, read and studied their English bibles, and kept alive the Wycliffite tenets on Church and sacraments. Some of these joined in an abortive rising in 1414 under Sir

John Oldcastle. After the quelling of this rebellion, Lollardy survived in pockets later in the century and beyond, providing a tenuous link with the sixteenth-century English Reformation.

Outside England knowledge of Wyclif's doctrines was widely spread among friends and foes. Because Richard II's Queen was from Bohemia, relations between the Universities of Oxford and Prague were close; Czech scholars copied Wyclif's manuscripts and carried them home. As Wyclif's manuscripts were destroyed in Oxford by the Archbishop's commissioners, they were recopied by scribes in Bohemia, and to this day more of them survive there than in England. In Bohemia John Hus preached doctrines very similar to those of Wyclif; they found congenial soil and flourished in conjunction with the Czechs' national aspirations to throw off the domination of German masters.

Wyclif's doctrines received their final formal condemnation by the universal Church at the Council of Constance, assembled in 1415, the year in which John of Gaunt's grandson, Henry V, won the battle of Agincourt. At the same Council Hus was tried and burnt, in violation of a safe-conduct; but the Hussites in Bohemia continued to resist suppression, and won a series of military victories under leaders of genius. The Hussites of Bohemia, much more than the Lollards in England, provided a kind of apostolic succession to link Wyclif with the Lutheran Reformation; a link acknowledged by Luther when he described Wyclif as a witness set up by God in advance to the truth of reformed doctrine.

In England it was the central role given to Wyclif by John Foxe in his *Book of Martyrs* that made him, in the mind of the Bible-reading Protestant, the John the Baptist of the Reformation. Henry VIII's break with the Papacy, and his abolition of the religious orders, carried out to the letter the reforms which Wyclif had advocated. Though Henry VIII retained the Mass and enforced belief in transubstantiation, and though Edward VI's bishops went further than Wyclif in the opposite direction in their denial of the real presence, Wyclif would have been content with the Eucharistic teaching of the settlement imposed under Elizabeth. At the end of her reign Bodley's librarian, Dr James, wrote a book to prove that Wyclif's teaching was in full accord with the thirty-nine articles.

From the sixteenth to the nineteenth century Wyclif was generally revered as a reformer and Bible translator, but his works were not much read or studied; his popularity waxed and waned, as now Low and now High Church was in the ascendant. Very few of his writings were in print, and his philosophy and systematic theology remained a closed book during the age of enlightenment.

So it continued until the nineteenth century. Robert Southey spoke for many when he said that Wyclif 'exercised himself in disputing against the Friars upon scholastic subtleties and questions which ending in nothing, as they begin, exercise the intellect without enriching it'. The revival of scholasticism in Catholic countries led to no new interest in Wyclif's philosophy: with all the volumes of Aquinas and Scotus to edit and digest there was not time to spare for the perusal of an infamous heretic. But the Wycliffite Bible was issued in a handsome edition in four volumes in 1850, and the English works attributed to him were published in three volumes between 1869 and 1871. Wyclif, along with the burnt bishops commemorated by the Martyr's Memorial, became a standard bearer of the Low Church party opposed to the Romanizing effects of the Oxford Movement, as the name of Wycliffe Hall in Oxford testifies to this day.

At last, in 1882, English students of the history of the
English language, and German Lutheran historians of
religion, came together to found the Wyclif Society, a group
of scholars which devoted itself for forty years to the
publication of the reformer's Latin works. Any student of
Wyclif today owes a great deal to the difficult and persisting
labours of the devoted scholars who produced over thirty
volumes of legible texts from crabbed manuscripts. But it
cannot be said that the publication of the Wyclif Society
volumes led to a great interest in Wyclif's systematic
writings. It was as if the learned world sank back with relief
when the Society's work was done. Honour was satisfied
now the man had been edited: no one could be expected
actually to read him. Even in his own college of Balliol
Wyclif, had he returned at the beginning of his centenary
year of 1984, would have found the pages of most of his
Latin works uncut.

J. A. Robson, whose book *Wyclif and the Oxford Schools*
(1961) is the most substantial treatment of Wyclif's
philosophy yet to have appeared, writes vividly of the
difficulties under which the Wyclif Society editors
laboured.

> The first was lack of knowledge of the background to
> Wyclif's works. Only in comparatively recent years has
> an intensive publication of texts and monographs
> enabled us to trace the development of thought in the
> universities of the fourteenth century. It was hard,
> therefore, convincingly to relate Wyclif's philosophical
> opinions to the age in which he lived . . . The second
> difficulty was self-imposed. It was the determination of
> the Wyclif Society editors to prove their subject a major
> original philosopher . . . It is amusing and disturbing to
> read Dziewicki's attempt to prove Wyclif's logic

superior to Ockham's and his opinion that, whilst his work has 'grave omissions' and his digressions 'go beyond all bounds', nevertheless 'without Ockham's affectation of mathematical order, Wyclif had as much of the true philosophical spirit as he; and as for subtlety and originality, he perhaps had more'.

Dziewicki's judgement of the relative merits of Wyclif's philosophy and Ockham's does not seem to me at all as bizarre as it did to Robson. It will not be until Wyclif's philosophical works have received some degree of the attention which has been accorded to Ockham's that we will be in a position to judge. But the time is ripe to begin a reappraisal of Wyclif's merits as a philosopher. After forty years of linguistic analysis, the methods and problems of Oxford philosophy today resemble the Oxford of the fourteenth century more than they resemble the Oxford of the heyday of British Hegelianism. Worldwide, the study of medieval philosophy, once the almost exclusive preserve of Catholic universities whose preoccupations were predominantly theological, has begun to interest professional philosophers who share an interest in the kind of problem which exercised Wyclif in his youth, and are not likely to be predisposed against him by the condemnations which fell upon him in his old age and after his death. Robson himself, who did a magnificent job in piecing together the structure of Wyclif's philosophical *summa*, was too distant by training from the type of philosophical concern which Wyclif shared with contemporary linguistic philosophers to form a just appreciation of his subject's philosophical merits; and when he wrote, Wyclif's major philosophical work, the *De Universalibus*, had not been published. It may well be that, if Wyclif had not become a heretic, he might have been remembered as one of a great triumvirate of Oxford scholastics along with Scotus and Ockham.

What of Wyclif's standing as a theologian? His role in the controversial ages of the sixteenth and nineteenth centuries was clear enough. In our own more ecumenical era, does he deserve attention, and, if so, what kind of attention?

It is clear that the editing of Wyclif gave qualms, of varying kinds, to his nineteenth-century Lutheran, Anglican, and Catholic editors. The Low Church subscribers to the Society no doubt enjoyed the polemical works, but must have been more and more dismayed as crabbed scholastic texts began to arrive through their letter boxes. Some of the editors were so sure that Wyclif was a good Lutheran that they would read Lutheran doctrine into the text where none was to be found. Thus in the *On The Truth of Scripture* we find Wyclif concluding a rather balanced treatment of the celibacy of the clergy by saying, 'It seems to me that if a priest is married he should refrain from intercourse with his wife, and indeed should not be ordained before he is released from his marital obligations.' Wyclif's editor Buddensieg valiantly inserts a marginal summary: 'Therefore a priest may marry'.

The Catholic Dziewicki, on the other hand, felt difficulties from the opposite quarter.

People have asked me many a time how I, nominally a Catholic, could aid in publishing the works of one so contrary to Catholicism as Wyclif is universally considered to be; and they readily supposed that I was indeed a Catholic only in name. They mistook; and though I have sincerely – and I hope successfully – tried to edit Wyclif with perfect impartiality from first to last, I have no sympathy with those of his doctrines that contradict the teaching of my Church. The facts are briefly as follows. When I was offered the position of editor of Wyclif's Latin works, I consulted a clergyman of my faith in London. He told me that a translation into the vernacular would be forbidden, but that a mere edition of the Latin text was quite another thing.

Since Wyclif's writings contain both the Catholic elements which disconcerted Buddensieg, and the Protestant elements which troubled Dziewicki, it is not, in fact, inappropriate to look on his work from an ecumenical viewpoint. In the reformer's centenary year we have seen produced the magnificent catalogue of his Latin writings, the work of scholars of two generations of the Thomson family. It is striking that this appears under the imprint of the Pontifical Institute of Medieval Studies.

If Wyclif were to return to England today he would find echoes of his teaching in more than one ecclesiastical tradition. Obviously, he would be proud to see how his reforming ideals continue to inspire churchmen of Protestant inspiration; but he would find even the adherents of the Church of Rome very different from the Catholics he knew. Boniface VIII's claims to universal lordship seem no less impudent to Catholics today than they did to Wyclif himself. John Paul II, unlike Gregory XI, has no divisions, and when Papal nuncios come to England it is not in order to collect taxes. Indeed, Wyclif might be surprised to discover that it was in the Roman Church, rather than in the establishment whose founders proclaimed him as their precursor, that there was to be found a disendowed clergy living, as he had recommended, on freely given alms.

Among all denominations Wyclif would discover the Bible freely available in the vernacular, with the laity as well as the clergy encouraged to read and study it. In both Roman and Anglican churches he would observe, no doubt to his dismay, that there were friars to be seen; but he would find that even in the Roman Church, and even among friars, Eucharistic doctrines were being defended very similar to those teachings of his own which had made the friars disown him. In the Roman Church, he would discover, it was now possible to question the infallibility of the Pope without incurring excommunication; and among the Anglican hierarchy there were those who sought communion with Christians who had abandoned that distinction between presbyter and bishop which he regarded as post-Apostolic.

In philosophy, too, Wyclif might find much that was congenial in surprising places. He would find that the issues which concerned him were debated not only in those Catholic institutions which explicitly draw inspiration from medieval models, but in secular universities which would feel quite alien the theological purposes to which he and his colleagues devoted their philosophical inquiries. In his own university he would encounter philosophers puzzling, as he did, over the nature of meaning and truth, existence and essence, and necessity and contingency; he would find that many people condemned these philosophers, as he condemned his own contemporaries, for being excessively concerned to reduce questions of substance to questions of language. He would no doubt be astonished to discover that of all his ideas the one most influential throughout the world of the twentieth century was the thesis that in an ideal world all ownership of property would be common ownership.

A returning Wyclif, then, would find that causes for which he had campaigned had won victories both among the successors of the Church he wished to reform, and among the successors of those who had departed from it to carry out the kinds of reform he advocated. But beyond doubt he would also feel that no Church had come far enough in the pursuit of the primitive and evangelical simplicity which he regarded as the Christian vocation. He would find that the philosophical battles in which he had spent his early years still needed to be fought, as throughout the learned world realists and anti-realists clash over the nature of truth and necessity. Reincarnate, he would no doubt throw himself with unaltered zeal into the old battles: worldliness must still be cast out in the *ecclesia semper reformanda*; the true philosopher must still defend divine metaphysics against the doctors of signs who would replace it with tinkling nominalism.

Further reading

There is no wholly satisfactory book dealing with the life and work of Wyclif. The standard biography was published in two volumes in 1926 by Herbert Workman under the title *John Wyclif: A study of the English Medieval Church*. This is a mine of information about the circumstances of Wyclif's career and the chronology of his activities, and it gives full details of anyone who ever crossed his path; but it is quite inadequate as an account of Wyclif's own philosophy or theology. The most accessible and popular book on the reformer is K. B. McFarlane's *John Wycliffe and the Beginnings of English Nonconformity* (1952). This is much more useful about the later Lollards than about Wyclif himself, with whom its author was greatly out of sympathy. J. A. Robson's *Wyclif and the Oxford Schools* (1951) is informative about the background to Wyclif's philosophical work and pieces together the evidence about the structure of his *summa*; but it is inadequate as an account of his thought. There has recently appeared an annotated catalogue of the Latin writings of Wyclif by Williell R. Thomson (1984), in part from the notes of his father, the late S. Harrison Thomson who was one of the most distinguished Wyclif scholars of the period between the wars. The chapter on Wyclif's thought in Gordon Leff's *Heresy in the Later Middle Ages* (1967), though sometimes open to philosophical criticism, is the best brief presentation of his main doctrines. An easily obtainable, and excellently annotated, selection of the English works attributed to Wyclif is Anne Hudson's *Selections from English Wycliffite Writings* (Cambridge University Press,

1978). The standard edition of almost all Wyclif's Latin works are the volumes of the Wyclif Society; they are quoted from those volumes by 'W' followed by the year of publication and the page reference.

Index

absenteeism, 58
accidents, 19, 82–6
annates, 44
annihilation, 28–9, 83
Antichrist, 62, 73–6, 98
Aquinas, 10, 39, 60, 87, 103
Aristotle, 4, 10, 12, 14–15, 47, 59
atomism, 4–5, 62
Augustine, St, 10, 16, 17, 82, 98
Avignon, 43–4, 56, 74–6

Ball, John, 92
Balliol, 3, 42, 99, 104
being, 9, 18–30
Berengar, 88
Bible, 52, 57–66, 103, 107
Blackfriars, 94, 97
bliss, 69–70
Boniface VIII, 71, 107
Bridget of Sweden, St, 74
Buddensieg, R., 106–7
Burley, W., 10, 11

Caim's castles, 94, 99
Cambalek, 75
canon of scripture, 61
cardinals, 93
Catherine of Siena, St, 74
celibacy, 105
Church, 51, 68–77
communism, 11, 46–7
confiscation, 44, 51
Constance, Council of, 57, 102
Constantine, 77
contingence, 33, 41

Courtenay, W., 53, 92, 94, 96
crusade, 98

damnation, 40, 64
Decretals, 62
Descartes, 86
dominion, 45–55, 70, 92
Dziewicki, M., 104–5, 107

endowment, 49, 51, 77
entity, 18, 22
essence, 21–2, 24, 26, 28
essential being, 18, 19–21
essential predication, 25
eternal truths, 34–5
Eucharist, 80–90
excommunication, 50
existence, 18–19, 22
extension, 85

Fitzralph, R., 3, 10
foreknowledge, 33–8, 40
form, 12
formal predication, 25
Foxe, John, 102
freedom, 31–41
friars, 2, 89, 93–5, 97

Gaunt, John of, 1, 52, 91
genus, 11, 12–13, 20
grace, 49–53, 70
Gregory XI, 43, 45, 53, 73–4
Grosseteste, 2, 10, 45, 98

habitudinal predication, 25
Henry VIII, 80, 102
host, 82–90

Hudson, A., 110
Hume, David, 24
Hus, John, 102

Ideas, 14, 18
indulgences, 72–3
inerrancy, 60
Ireland, 85

kings, 48, 51, 77–9
Knox, R. A., 100
Koran, 62

Lateran Council, 88
law, 47
Leff, G., 110
linguistic philosophy, 5–7, 105, 108
logic, 3–4, 22, 59
logical universals, 15
Lollards, 95–6, 101–2
lordship, 45–55
Luther, 102, 106
Lutterworth, 66, 93, 98–9
lying, 63–4

Macaulay, Lord, 56
metaphysical universals, 18
metaphysics, 18
monarchy, 48

necessity, 31–41
Newman, J. H., 100–1
Nicholas of Hereford, 66, 94–6
nominalism, 6–17

Ockham, William, 1, 3, 8, 10, 91, 105
Old Testament, 63, 71
Oldcastle, Sir J., 102

pacifism, 97–8
Peasants' Revolt, 92

permission, 35–6
Peter, St, 37, 50, 66, 73–5
phenomenalism, 85
Plato, 14–15, 47
Popes, 50–5, 57, 71–6
possession, 45–6
predestination, 31, 39, 40, 68
predication, 11–13, 25–6
presentiality, 38
privations, 26
provisions, 43–5
Purvey, John, 66

qualities, 84
quantifiers, 22–3
quiddity, 21

real presence, 80–90, 103
real proposition, 11
realism, 6–17
Repton, Philip, 94–6
Rigg, Robert, 94
Robert of Geneva, 56, 76
Robson, W., 104–5, 110
Rome, 74–5
roses, 20–1

sanctuary, 67
schism, 55, 75–6
scholasticism, 100, 103
Scotus, Duns, 1, 3, 91, 103
scripture, 52, 60–4
Silvester, St, 77, 99
similarity, 15–16
slavery, 48
Southey, Robert, 103
species, 11–12, 18, 20–1
substance, 81–90

taxation, 43–4
Thomson, S. H., 107, 110
tithes, 51
tradition, 61

transubstantiation, 80–90, 103
Trent, Council of, 81, 87
truth, 6, 20

universals, 7–17
Urban V, 42
Urban VI, 54–5, 57, 68, 74, 76

war, 98
Wesley, John, 100–1
Workman, H., 110
Wyclif, John, works:
   On Apostasy, 82, 93
   On Blasphemy, 93
   On the Church, 67–73, 77
   On Civil Dominion, 45–55,
    70, 77, 92
   On the Divine Commands,
    45

On Divine Dominion, 43
On the Eucharist, 82–90
*On the Incarnation of the
  Word*, 43
*The Mirror of Secular
  Lords*, 64
On the Office of King, 68,
  77–9
Opus Evangelicum, 98
Sermons, 96
On Simony, 93
On the State of Innocence,
  45
Summa de Ente, 96
Trialogue, 97
*On the Truth of Sacred
  Scripture*, 57–64, 67
On Universals, 7–41
Wyclif Society, 9, 104

OXFORD

MORE PAST MASTERS

Details of a selection of other Past Masters follow. A complete list of Oxford Paperbacks, including The World's Classics, Twentieth-Century Classics, OPUS, Oxford Authors, Oxford Shakespeare, and Oxford Paperback Reference, as well as Past Masters, is available from the General Publicity Department, Oxford University Press, Walton Street, Oxford OX2 6DP.

In the USA, complete lists are available from the Paperbacks Marketing Manager, Oxford University Press, 200 Madison Avenue, New York, NY 10016.

AQUINAS Anthony Kenny

Anthony Kenny writes about Thomas Aquinas as a philosopher, for readers who may not share Aquinas's theological interests and beliefs. He begins with an account of Aquinas's life and works, and assesses his importance for contemporary philosophy. The book is completed by more detailed examinations of Aquinas's metaphysical system and his philosophy of mind.

'It is hard to see how such a book could be done better.' *London Review of Books*

THOMAS MORE Anthony Kenny

The place of Thomas More in the intellectual history of Europe is secure, but a fair judgement of the man and his works is made difficult by the varied and biased criticism to which they have been exposed. Dr Kenny argues in this book that Thomas More's life presents a coherent character whose qualities can and should be admired, even by those who do not share his beliefs.

'a small masterpiece' Norman St John-Stevas, Books of 1983, *Sunday Times*

BAYLE Elisabeth Labrousse

French Protestantism found its most commanding voice in Pierre Bayle, a remarkable seventeenth-century writer and philosopher who was driven by religious intolerance to exile in Holland. Elisabeth Labrousse shows how his philosophy and religious doctrine developed in relation to both of the main intellectual traditions—the Christian and the sceptical—that influenced his generation. She reveals the importance of his best-known work, the *Dictionary*, and explores his views on such questions as religious toleration and evil.

'Excellently translated by Denys Potts, Labrousse's clever, historically sensitive book is a model of clarity and distinction.' *Sunday Times*

PASCAL Alban Krailsheimer

Alban Krailsheimer opens his study of Pascal's life and work with a description of Pascal's religious conversion, and then discusses his literary, mathematical, and scientific achievements, which culminated in the acute analysis of human character and the powerful reasoning of the *Pensées*. He argues that after his conversion Pascal put his previous work in a different perspective and saw his, and in general all, human activity in religious terms.

'Mr Krailsheimer's enthusiasm is eloquent and infectious.' *Observer*